MISS BECKY'S
CHARM SCHOOL

D0328712

MISS BECKY'S CHARM SCHOOL

Using Southern Belle Secrets to Land Your Man

Becky Rutledge, Ph.D.

CITADEL PRESS
Kensington Publishing Corp.
www.kensingtonbooks.com

CITADEL PRESS BOOKS are published by

Kensington Publishing Corp.
850 Third Avenue
New York, NY 10022

All Kensington titles, imprints, and distributed lines are available at
special quantity discounts for bulk purchases for sales promotions,
premiums, fund-raising, educational, or institutional use. Special book
excerpts or customized printings can also be created to fit specific needs.
For details, write or phone the office of the Kensington special sales
manager: Kensington Publishing Corp., 850 Third Avenue, New York,
NY 10022, attn: Special Sales Department; phone 1-800-221-2647.

First printing: August 2007

10 9 8 7 6 5 4 3 2 1

Printed in the United States of America

Library of Congress Control Number: 2007922608

ISBN-13: 978-0-8065-2825-0
ISBN-10: 0-8065-2825-7

Dedication

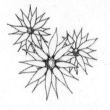

To all girls everywhere—

you deserve the best,

so go and get it!

Contents

Introduction

I was born in the South, raised in the South, and have lived in the South all my life. I am married to a Southerner, and a pretty handsome one at that! Although I have traveled all over the world, nothing feels like home as much as being here—in the South.

What makes us so special, you may ask? It's hard to put into a nice, neat little package, but I'll try. We *are* different down here—from the way we talk, laugh, and sing, to the way we think.

One thing here about how we talk: We talk *a lot*! Southerners have been said to never know a stranger. That's because by the time you make it through the grocery store line, you know all about the lady in front of you—her husband's preference for beans over asparagus, her nasty cold, and her weekend plans! It doesn't matter that you may never see her again. That's not the point. We are simply friendly, engaging people.

Now I might be biased, but I do believe people in the South are more sentimental as a rule. What we carry in our memories is different, and that might explain a lot about why we love to tell stories. What is really a three-minute story can easily be drawn out to five or seven minutes, complete with a good bit of embellishment and humor, if a Southerner is doing the talking!

I became a psychologist in part because of my Southern heritage. I was taught that people are intriguing, and if you listen very closely, they all have tales to tell. Relationships are particularly fun to observe as partners dance and squirm in all sorts of directions to make another person happy. And Southerners love anything that is "family."

You will notice that I try to be funny about the subject of getting a man. You may also notice that I poke fun at the South, its ways and its inhabitants. Why? Well, first, the process of getting a man is just plain funny, don't you think? And second, if you can't laugh at yourself, you are going to be one unhappy camper for the rest of your life!

I was raised in a Methodist home, and went to an all-girl Catholic prep school. You probably don't care to know this, but I *am* getting ready to make a point. There was this one nun, Sister Agnes Ricarda, who had to be 180 years old because she had been there forever! Every Friday before we left for the weekend, she would say, "Remember girls, don't sell yourself short." Actually, I think she was trying to warn us to behave over the weekend and not to "put out." Nonetheless, as I have grown up (a little), I think of it in a different way. Each of us has something special to offer someone else. But if we don't recognize it, no one else will either. So my biggest advice to you as you start down the road to nailing a man is to never, ever sell yourself short!

The point of this book is pretty simple. There are some tried-and-true techniques that work when it comes to getting a man, and you can read all about them here. Enjoy yourself. Let me know how you like it or how you didn't, but I might have one big hissy fit if you send really nasty mail!

Here's my website: www.askdrbecky.com. Go to it and find out what's going on—and to tell me about your experiences. I look forward to hearing from you.

MISS BECKY'S CHARM SCHOOL

CHAPTER ONE

Honey, What Is It You Want Him For?

Women rule the world, but it's supposed to be a secret.

—Molly Haskell

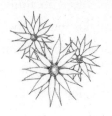

If you are ready to snag a man Southern belle style, there are a few things you need to know before you get started. Sidlin' up to the buffet without knowing what you're after can get you in a heap of trouble! Before you go after what you want, doesn't it make sense to narrow your focus by doing a little research? Whether hunting for a boyfriend, a husband, or something in between, there are plenty of breeds to pick from.

Relationships and men are like ships (actually, down here in the South, we call them plain ol' boats, but ships sounds better). You can ride the waves of romance on many different kinds of ships, or you can pick one ship and cruise along. But picking the type of ship you want can be tricky. Most men can be found somewhere between the Disney Big Red Boat (think twelve-year-ol' mentality) and the *Titanic* (totally disabled). So what sort of "ship" do you want to launch? Platonic? Passion with no commitment? Just a good date? A mate?

Sometimes you get on one kind of "ship" and you think you like where it's going, but then you end up going in a completely different direction. Y'all need to think about what kind of a "relation-ship" would make you happy *right now*. We girls from the South believe you deserve the best, and it's up to you to decide what that might be. Let's get started by answering a few questions. Circle the one with which you most identify.

1. *In terms of a man's physical appearance, I . . .*

    a. Want a man so hot that you could fry an egg on his behind.
    b. Want a man who is long and lean, with slow hands and a soft touch.
    c. Want a man who is cute, but no cuter than I am.
    d. Want a man who appreciates how long it takes to get dressed.
    e. Want a man with good genes who looks good in those tight jeans!

2. *Are "smarts" important?*

    a. Only to the extent he doesn't embarrass himself in public.
    b. Yes, but only when it comes to finding my G-spot.
    c. He should be as smart as I am and he should "get" me.
    d. Not really, he just needs to be smart enough to adore me!
    e. Hell, yes!

3. *Is money important?*

    a. Not as much as the appearance of having it.
    b. Only to the extent it will cover the cost of a room and room service.

    c. As long as we can split the tab, it's not important.

    d. It's about how he spends it rather than what he has.

    e. Yes! I want to drive the nicest damn minivan in the carpool line!

4. *If I could be anywhere with a man, I'd be . . .*

    a. The envy of all of my friends at the hottest party in town.

    b. In bed.

    c. Watching a movie that *I* picked out, and eating popcorn.

    d. Antiquing and picking out stemware from Pier One.

    e. Shopping for wedding bands and child-friendly neighborhoods.

5. *When I'm out to dinner with a man . . .*

    a. I expect him to cater to whatever I want.

    b. Who cares? Dinner is only the "appetizer" for the evening ahead!

    c. I want fun company and comfort food.

    d. I want to be able to discuss the food presentation and what's in the recipe.

    e. Whatever *he* would enjoy is fine with me.

6. *If I made more money than a man, I would expect him to . . .*

    a. Enjoy the ride.

    b. Be appreciative of my 1,500-thread-count Egyptian cotton sheets.

    c. Let me pick up the dinner tab now and then.

    d. Go on a shopping spree with me.

    e. Work it out if it were an issue for him.

7. *I want a man who finds me at my most attractive when* . . .

    a. He feels like *he* is the most attractive!

    b. I'm on his mind.

    c. I'm at my most needy.

    d. I am concerned about being pretty.

    e. I am knee-deep in whatever it is I am doing at the moment.

8. *I have to buy a new car. My man* . . .

    a. Encourages me to buy the fastest and hottest car around so he can borrow it.

    b. Wants me to buy a car with a big backseat.

    c. Is all about practicality and helping me get the best car for the money.

    d. Wants the car to reflect who I am and that matches my pretty little eyes and hair color.

    e. Wants me to have a car I would enjoy driving as long as it's safe.

9. *If I got a speeding ticket, while driving my man's car* . . .

    a. He wouldn't care.

    b. I wouldn't dare drive his car—someone might recognize me!

    c. He would worry about my insurance rates.

d. He would be outraged and horrified for me, and then help me fight it.

e. He would insist that I go to driving school to avoid paying higher insurance.

10. *If I were having a crying spell, my man would . . .*

a. Run.

b. Put me to bed and "comfort" me.

c. Be there for me "just in case" I needed comforting.

d. Bring me a box of tissues, a stack of my favorite chick flicks, and a tub of chocolate chunk ice cream.

e. Brainstorm logical ways to fix the problem.

11. *For my birthday, my man would . . .*

a. Do whatever I want because I'm paying for it.

b. Grant my every naughty wish!

c. Help me celebrate however I wish.

d. Treat me to a deluxe mani/pedi.

e. Top what he's done for birthdays past.

12. *A perfect vacation with a man would be . . .*

a. Anywhere that's fun.

b. In a location that requires little socializing and a *lot* of fantasy fulfillment.

c. Camping and sex—but only if we both feel like it!

d. At an exclusive spa—his treat.

e. A cruise that includes all the things *I* like.

13. *If my man had a pet . . .*

    a. He wouldn't. He's too busy going out to have time for pets.

    b. He'd have an aquarium.

    c. He'd have a mutt he rescued from the pound.

    d. He'd have a cat.

    e. He'd have a Lab.

14. *If I were to meet his parents . . .*

    a. I have no need whatsoever to meet his parents.

    b. It would only be by accident.

    c. They would treat me like one of their own.

    d. I'd be his "cover" girlfriend.

    e. I'd be nervous as a whore in church!

15. *If I were to meet his friends . . .*

    a. I'd be bored with them.

    b. I doubt I'd ever meet any of his friends.

    c. I'd be seen as "one of the guys."

    d. I'd be the queen bee.

    e. I'd be treated like a treasure.

16. *The most important thing a man needs to know about me is . . .*

    a. How to make me look good.

    b. What makes me feel sexiest.

    c. My favorite ice cream.

    d. My shoe size.

    e. What makes me tick.

17. *I need a man who will . . .*

    a. "Show good" like a hog at the county fair.

    b. Know when it's time to go home.

    c. Have no expectations about the future.

    d. Fit in with the girls.

    e. Be the man I can count on to do what a man's supposed to do.

You're probably wondering what some of these questions mean and how in the world it would help with your research. Read on, read on, for you are going to see what "ship" you're about to set sail on!

Mostly a's: If you picked mostly a's, you want the *"Oh my God, he's so hot, like Matthew McConaughey dipped in homemade ice cream, I can hardly breathe because if I do I might go into cardiac arrest!"-ship*. Girls, this is what I like to call your eye candy. You've heard of men who have "hood ornaments" or "trophy wives," haven't you? Well, you, too, can have a hood ornament if that's what *you* want or need.

A hood ornament is handsome, personable, and knows how to act at a party! Like I said in the quiz, he "shows good," and can work a room just by walking into it. He doesn't have to be smart as long as he can make what we call "cocktail conversation." He is shallow, but in the nicest possible way—just don't expect him to be able to handle any heavy emotional stuff. He is the man who makes you the envy of all the other women in the room and makes you feel fantastic about yourself. In other words, he is the target, but you, my dear, are the bull's eye! Of course, he probably spends more time on his looks and getting ready than you do, but who cares? He is gorgeous, but he is *all about you*! And the best part of it is this: Guys are like dogs, and I mean this in a good way. If one dog has a treat, all the other dogs just seem to naturally want that treat, too. And in this case, *you* are the treat!

My personal version of the hood ornament is tall, lean, and tan. His steely blue eyes look right through you and leave your stomach in a little knot. He knows just how to walk beside you with his hand at the small of your back . . . oh sorry, I'm getting carried away by my fantasy. Back to work . . .

True, this guy is gorgeous. And even though he may not be the brightest bulb in the bunch, remember one thing: He may be a little dumb, but he's not stupid. He's still a guy with a penis and an ego, so be careful about how you approach him.

Take my friend JoBeth (yep that's her real name!). She met her hottie—a twenty-year-old man who was tall and lean—at her brother's barbecue. Steven—with a *v*—was the best dancer in town and looked better in a suit or tux than anyone we knew. He loved the social scene but, since he was new to town, he didn't get out much. JoBeth didn't want a strings-attached relationship at the time, and Steven was an aspiring actor (read: a waiter) who needed some experience, so she concocted a three-step plan.

Steven had a motorcycle and couldn't stop talking about it. JoBeth could give a rat's $#* about Harleys, but she pretended real well (#1). He took the bait and bought her a helmet, gloves, and boots. JoBeth felt "just awful" that he had spent a week's pay on her and told him so (#2). She wanted to make it up to him somehow so she offered to help with his "acting" career (#3). She would take him to Saks and pay for a Giorgio Armani suit in exchange for his being her date to a bunch of Christmas parties. It was a match made in heaven.

You have to understand JoBeth a little here. Her daddy divorced her mama when she was about fifteen. He's been married four times now and, with each new union, the ornament gets younger and younger. This last whippersnapper he married is JoBeth's age! When JoBeth commented about this, her daddy told her that "she makes me feel young and attractive." Since JoBeth has always been a daddy's girl, she decided she wanted to see what the stir was all about.

Not long ago, me and the girls were invited to a high-falutin' party at the club. As we were checking out the crowd, in walked JoBeth. Of course, she looked fantastic, but that's not what we noticed. It was *him*! In all my born days I've never seen anything like this most gorgeous, tall drink of water. We were all so blown away by him that we were speechless, and believe me, that is definitely not characteristic of us. She introduced us to Steven and before you knew it we were giggling, stammering, and generally acting like teenagers. His smile was slightly transparent, but oh my goodness, his teeth were soooo white. She smiled demurely at him and asked if he could get her a drink. He kissed her cheek, winked, tossed us an infectious grin, and was off to the bar like a beagle after a rabbit. JoBeth immediately launched into how she met him and what she was up to, but no one cared. All we wanted to know is where we could get one. And did he have a brother???

Mostly b's: You say you picked mostly b's? Then you might want the *"Paul will be here in an hour; I need more time to put something sexy together, and I wonder if we'll even make it to dinner?"-ship*. This, y'all, is your very sexy, makes-you-weak-in-the-knees lover. The sexual tension is electrifying, and you may have a few things in common, but there's not much more to it—and that's enough for this "deal." Neither of you is interested in a relationship that requires commitment, emotional intimacy, or any other of that time-consuming stuff.

This relationship is your delicious secret. His job is to be available when you want him, and to please you like you've never been pleased before. When he looks at you, he's undressing you with his eyes. Intelligence is really not necessary here since you're not going to be discussing quantum physics—your conversations consist mostly of witty banter and sexual innuendo. And there's no need for you to introduce him to your friends—in fact, his smoldering sexuality is the very reason you haven't seen as much of your friends as usual. You will definitely enjoy him, but you don't feel compelled to explain it.

Caroline has always been a no-nonsense kind of Southern belle. She spends so much time at her law practice that we hardly ever see her, so she has even less time for the demands of a boyfriend. Until she met her "special friend" Thomas, Caroline had never worn anything but sensible white panties and cotton bras. Not too long ago, she called me to go shopping with her. I was thrilled—a Southern lady never passes up an opportunity to see her friends and to shop! You could've knocked me over with a feather when she stopped in front of Victoria's Secret and suggested we go in. She spent God knows how much money on these tiny silk thongs and matching lacy push-up bras. Then we went all over hell's half-acre to find the perfect pair of stilettos because she'd heard they would make her thighs look thinner. All I could do was stare at her—who was this person and what had she done to my friend? When I called her last Wednesday to go out for fried chicken, she was too busy shaving her legs, lotioning her body, and picking out her lingerie getup for Thomas that night. It's downright exasperating, if you ask me. Or maybe I'm just jealous. Caroline gets to have great sex, and sends him home afterward so that she can down a half-pint of chocolate chip ice cream alone in bed. Really, it's just not fair! I mean, it's been six weeks since I've seen Caroline and has she even bothered to introduce me?

Of course, this type of arrangement can get complicated, especially if one of you starts to develop feelings for the other. The rules of this type of "ship" imply that there won't be any emotional commitment, and that neither of you has to be monogamous. That leaves little room for possessiveness or jealousy. When these rules are broken, someone is likely to get hurt, so be careful!

Mostly c's: If you answered mostly c's, then perhaps you need the *"Yeah, I've been drinking, I haven't brushed my teeth all day, and* *my face is still in the cabinet, but sure—come on over"-ship*. This, my friends, is the "buddy with benefits." First and foremost, he is a friend. If you are needy, he can be counted on to be there for you with a pint of your favorite Ben and Jerry's in tow. He is practical, he worries about you, and he has no unrealistic expectations about your relationship. The two of you can stay home and watch a movie, or you can hang out with friends. Your friendship is based on equality, so you each pay your own way. His friends consider you to be "one of the guys." You can ask him if your butt looks big in your new jeans and he'll actually tell you the truth. Sound a little boring? Think again. This relationship *does* have benefits, if you know what I mean. The sex is not a one-night stand. While it doesn't always have to be particularly hot, it's usually easy and comforting. Sex is not an issue in this relationship, but it's not a problem, either. There's simply no obligation to have sex but, if you do, there's no guilt.

Bob and Mary Kate have been friends since college. They have been through a lot together, and their friendship is more important than lemonade and sunshine. Bob has nursed Mary Kate through several breakups that she didn't handle particularly well. He recounted to us that after one boyfriend dumped her, she didn't bathe for a week, never changed her clothes, and her hair was so matted he had to help her cut some of the lumps out! But he was there and never left her, bless his soul. They have even vacationed together. Bob's parents include Mary Kate in get-togethers and have even designated one of the bedrooms in their house as her "home away from home." The sex between them is not frequent, but it has been a part of their relationship off and on for years. The only problem is when one of them is dating. Bob and Mary Kate continue their friendship whether they are in other relationships or not, and, of course, they don't have sex when dating other people. But many potential "keepers" have been intimidated by their bond and find it hard to compete. I mean, just imagine being Bob's new girlfriend, going to dinner to meet his buddy, Mary Kate. Over appetizers, they share inside jokes and finish each other's sentences. When you finally get the gumption to jump in and try saying something witty, Mary Kate gives Bob the "Where in tarnation did you find this one?" look.

I must warn you, however. This type of relationship can become so comfortable that you don't want to look for another relationship. This is not necessarily a bad thing, but be sure you aren't settling for "Mr. Okay for Now" just because it's easier than getting out there and finding "Mr. Right."

Mostly d's: For those of you who picked mostly d's, it sounds like you're on the *"Girlfriend, let's go out for margaritas and then we'll shop for antiques and look at boys!"-ship.* Every Southern girl knows the value of having a fabulous gay friend. It's the second best thing next to having a best girlfriend. Although it might be a stereotype, most gay men I know love to have lunch, shop, gossip, and are endlessly fascinated by your hair color, your waxing rituals, your shoes, and your jewelry. His companionship is immeasurable, and he always finds you funny. His friends think you are positively fabulous, and when you're with him, you're a true queen bee! On the few occasions you've met his ultraconservative parents, you've found yourself pretending that your relationship with him is something different, but you don't mind doing a favor for a friend. When you are down to the last bits of spare change in the bottom of your spent-too-much-on-it-but-had-to-have-it Kate Spade, he'll always pick up the tab. Other times, you pay the way. It is a nonstop adoration fest between the two of you!

My niece, Kelly, had a best friend named Sebastian while she lived in New York City. They had this instant connection. They spent all of their nonworking time shopping, eating at all of the best restaurants, going to the theater, and of course, checking out the hot guys. Sebastian sent her flowers for no reason—and she didn't even have to shave her legs! The relationship was blissful—that is, until Sebastian had the nerve to find the love of his life! Kelly was thrilled for him, but she had a hard time coming to terms with the fact that in order for Sebastian to have a successful relationship with his boyfriend, it meant he had to "break up" with her first. So be warned, if you are looking for a life of happiness with your gay man. The popular saying "All the good men are either taken or gay" will surely prove it to be true. Except in your case, the good men will be taken *and* gay!

Mostly e's: If you picked mostly e's, you probably want a more permanent arrangement: the *"I can see us growing old together, rocking on the porch, and playing with our grandchildren"-ship*. This is the man who wants you to pursue your dreams and is your biggest fan. He thinks the way you snort when you laugh is adorable. In other words, he thinks you hung the moon and wants to make you happy for the rest of your life!

This is *the* mate, the husband material, the man you flip over so badly that you find yourself writing your name with *his* last name on a napkin "just to see how it would look"! That's all well and good, but remember one of the cardinal rules: Southern belles know that appearances aren't everything. That blackberry patch may be tempting, but the juiciest fruit is often found in its thorniest thicket, and often the one who is described as "just not your type" is the very one with whom you fall in love.

He may have some characteristics of each of the categories, but you find that they all blend together into one amazing man. Unlike the hood ornament, you discover that you have a lot in common. Unlike the hot lover, he finds out what makes you feel loved—in *and* out of the bedroom—and then he does it. He treats your best friend like a queen even though he doesn't understand half of what the two of you are discussing. His friends welcome you into their circle. When it comes time to meet his parents, you really *are* nervous as a whore in church!

Mary (pronounced down here as "Maaaaary") grew up in Atlanta and fancies herself quite the high-class, educated, sophisticated belle. She always dated nothing but wealthy, eligible bachelors from the country club that her parents belong to, and, if I may say so myself, she is a bit of a snob. So imagine my shock when she called to announce she was engaged to a fella who was nowhere to be found on the social register! Now, I always love a good wedding, but I have had about enough of those bridesmaids' gowns designed especially to make you look less attractive than the bride! I had images of a frou-frou wedding with twenty bridesmaids in pink tulle gowns and was not looking forward to that! But I digress.

Mary met TJ (short for Thomas, Junior) when she was at a spa in Arkansas. If you're laughing right now, I have to wonder if it's because she fell in love with a guy from Arkansas or because she actually went to a spa in Arkansas! Anyway, get this: TJ's family owns a big ol' pig farm! Evidently, it's quite a grueling business, so TJ was at the spa for some relaxation. In addition to the fact that he's a pig farmer, he doesn't look anything like the men Mary had been attracted to in the past. Now I've got nothing against the less-than-handsome man, but poor TJ. He is shorter than my ever-shrinking granny, and is about two-thirds of the way toward total baldness. He is also, regrettably, a bit pudgy. But despite all that, when I went to a pig roast on his farm to celebrate their engagement, I have to say I have never seen a couple so in love or a fiancé so attentive. Ironically, Mary has this annoying habit of squealing like a stuck pig when she gets excited. But then I guess TJ is probably already used to such noises. I like thinking that it doesn't bother him, I'm sure he embraces the best and worst of my friend. In fact, I think he actually *does* believe she hung the moon. I just hope she likes life on a pig farm, bless her heart.

Now that you have an idea of what type of *relationship* into which you are prepared to invest, the second piece of research is to decide what *type* of man you prefer. There are about as many choices as there are flavors of ice cream, so let's get started.

Top 5 Reasons a Southern Belle Needs a Man

1 Those doors just won't open themselves.

2 A girl shouldn't have to buy her own lobster.

3 Sometimes it's easier than calling a repairman.

4 It's just too cold (too rainy, too hot . . .) to pump your own gas.

5 It keeps my mama from asking too many questions.

CHAPTER TWO

Separating the Possums from the Bunnies

*Only a Southerner both knows and understands the difference
between a redneck, a good ol' boy, and po' white trash.*

—Anonymous

There are about as many types of men as there are furry little creatures on this great, green earth. Big ones, short ones, fat and skinny, stupid and wise, rich and poor. Speaking of rich and poor, let me tell you what Southern mothers have taught their daughters: It's just as easy to fall in love with a rich man as a poor man. On the other hand, the same mothers might tell you that when you marry money, "you earn every penny of it!"

Anyway, out of that wide, vast herd of men out there, you have to know what kind of man you are *not* attracted to, so you can slim your pickin's to a more manageable size. Figuring out a man is like nailing jelly to a tree, so I enlisted a couple of my girlfriends, with the promise of free drinks, to come up with our Southern favorites. Now you need to know I mean no disrespect to any particular man, but we have to be able to label them somehow, so please excuse me if I offend anyone. I'm willing to betcha that wherever you live, you can identify some of these guys.

There is an important little lesson I must impart to you before going any further. In the South, little girls are taught that the way to spot a good man (a.k.a. "good husband material") is to check out how he treats his mama. Most of us laughed at that when we were too young to know better, but we learned our lesson later on.

Why do you need to know how to separate a great man from a not-so-great one? First, so you can better define what you want. Second and most important, you'll be able to look at a man, size him up rather quickly, and know whether you want to avoid him or get closer. So while I'm giving you a primer on the types of men out there, I'll also explain to you their relationships to their mamas and you can see firsthand that, dang it, this mama-rule *was* right!

THE REDNECK

Wade is a fine example of our first specimen—a **Redneck**. While Wade might be country as a turnip green, he doesn't have to live in the country to belong to this herd. The Redneck has no time for listening to others and what they think, and he's not out to impress anyone or put on airs. With the Redneck, what you see is what you get. This is the guy who has a fierce loyalty to the Old South, and expresses his pride by displaying the Rebel flag prominently somewhere on his truck. He loves women and, to prove it, he'll probably have a chrome metal female cutout on his mud flaps. He has adopted his views on things based on what he was taught, so he doesn't have the sense God gave him to have an independent thought, bless his soul. He sees himself as a God-fearing man but has little tolerance for anyone who isn't like him.

His idea of high fashion is to wear white socks with every outfit along with a camouflage shirt from the sporting goods store. His jeans don't fit quite right, and if you're lucky (or not), when he bends over you can see almost all the way to Texas. He buys his underwear in threepacks ($8.95) from the local Wal-Mart, and the "spit can" for his Redman chew is never far from his side when he's driving. The Redneck isn't concerned with superficial outside appearances. He doesn't own a suit. He cleans his nails with a pocketknife.

A Redneck treats his mama with respect, but he was raised by his daddy to know that the man is the King of the House, and he lives strictly by this rule. His mama was the type who stayed home and took care of everything while Daddy was at work. She expected dinner to be on the table at a certain hour and wanted everyone present. She always had the laundry and housework done before Daddy got home, and when he arrived, the TV remote was set right next to the Naugahyde recliner along with a cold beer. Mama did most of the raising of those little hellions on her own. Most of her discipline came in the form of, "Joe Ray, you better get your butt in here or I'll have to tell your daddy."

The Redneck adheres to the Southern expression of "Just 'cause I made it don't mean you can spend it." He won't think twice about buying a $6,000 four-wheeler but he'll give you hell for wasting thirty bucks on an electric can opener. Even if he could help it, he wouldn't see the need for change and that means you can't change him, either. Ladies, this guy is set in his ways, and if you can love him for that, then you'll do okay.

So what can you expect from your very own Redneck? I'm not

saying he'll be mean because he won't, but he doesn't have much of a feminine side. It's not his fault—he just doesn't know any better. He'll expect you to be as excited as he is about his deer hunting, fishing, new wide-screen TV, and whatever happened at work that day. When you don't show gushing enthusiasm, he won't get it. He just doesn't understand the difference between the sexes at all. His idea of romance is to grab you from behind and mutter, "Hey, baby, how 'bout some sugar?" On your anniversary, he'll proudly present you with a matching set of camouflage bra and panties. Girls, he ain't paying attention to that stuff and you'd be better off not to expect much else from him. One other thing, he is the jealous type—he doesn't want to see you dancing, talking, or looking in the direction of another man. You belong to him and no one else should mess with his honey!

Don't get me wrong—he's difficult, but just because he's difficult doesn't mean he's a bad guy! But he's definitely not the type of guy a girl with "high society" on her mind will go for. The Redneck is exactly how he presents himself to you. He's not full of surprises so, if this works for you, he may be perfect. He will love *you*, but all that other stuff—fancy panties and jewelry—just doesn't matter.

THE GOOD OL' BOY

My friend, Big L is a **Good Ol' Boy**. I've known Big L for years and he hasn't changed a whit. His needs are simple: if given the choice, he'd rather be hunting or fishing. One of his favorite destinations is the Bass Pro Shop. For those of you who may be unfamiliar with Bass Pro, it is a humongous sporting goods store where you can buy anything you can imagine for the fisherman, hunter, and camper. If they don't have it, you don't need it. Anyway, this man is more comfortable outside communing with nature and the boys. At any other time, he prefers to stay around home. You won't find him anywhere near the kitchen. He prefers to stay in the background while his wife, Darlene, takes care of the company, doing girlie duties like servin' up the appetizers and making small talk. But he can build one helluva fire, and that man can cook the most melt-in-your-mouth steaks on the grill.

Big L eats with his mouth closed, but he hasn't mastered keeping his elbows off the table and refraining from shoveling his food in like a pig at the trough. His views of women fall on the traditional side. He prefers a gal who isn't flashy and who is happy pursuing whatever makes her little heart sing! But I have to give Big L credit. While the redneck could care less what others think unless it agrees with what *he* thinks, a Good Ol' Boy *will* listen to what others say, and he will offer up his own opinion when the occasion arises. Big L has a good heart and, under the right conditions, I've seen his tough exterior melt.

Believe it or not, Big L has an extremely deep, but private, relationship with his wife, Darlene. He adores her. But Darlene knows the true secret to making it work with a Good Ol' Boy: While she *can* influence him, she *can't* change him. You gotta love Big L because there's really nothing not to love.

As you might suspect, Big L reveres his mama. And any man

who reveres his mama will probably feel the same about you. For a Good Ol' Boy, meeting a woman as terrific as you are is a big surprise. He simply cannot believe his good fortune. Unlike the Redneck, he is much more thoughtful, more doting, and more aware of the treasure he has in you.

Your independence and fiery spirit is admired by men like Big L. He will see you as the epitome of womanhood just like his mama. In this relationship, it's okay for you to have a career. The Good Ol' Boy will be respectful of that and even supportive. He just won't be that into hearing about it or gung ho about giving you advice. He is way more proud of your domestic prowess!

THE RABBLE ROUSER

My friend Lilly dates Johnny. He is what we call a **Rabble Rouser**. Fun is his top priority. He's an acceptable dresser, and is somewhat smart. He likes things mostly clean and orderly, but his favorite activity is raisin' hell. Johnny stays out all weekend with the boys, but during the week he's home with Lilly. Although his carousing makes her madder than a hornet, she can't help but like him because he's full of excitement and mischief. He keeps a tab at the local bar in their neighborhood, and he's been known to jump behind the counter and serve up the beer for his buddies. He's also the one who's always yelling for some Lynyrd Skynyrd music. He's not happy unless there is a little trouble brewing somewhere and rules are being broken. He's a practical joker—

he's the one with the remote-control fart machine, who'll use it at the most inopportune time!

Johnny loves a party and is usually smack-dab in the middle of it, drunker than Cooter Brown. Every year he's at the Grove in Oxford, Mississippi, for the Ole Miss/Mississippi State game, and his tailgating parties are legendary. His antics and running wild are not intended to hurt Lilly, but he can't seem to control himself. Why does Lilly put up with him? Because she can't resist his little-boy grin and his easy charm. He may never grow up, but hell's fire, he sure is a lot of fun! And, when he is with Lilly, she gets to be the center of his universe, and he treats her like a queen.

So what can you expect if you're this guy's gal? A Rabble Rouser is the type of guy for whom Mother's Day was created. The only reason he remembers Mother's Day or her birthday is because his little sister reminds him. Don't get me wrong, he loves his mama but, if it's not all about him, then it's not on his radar. So he goes through the motions and gets the flowers, the perfect Hallmark card, and whatever else he is "supposed to do." His mama forgives his attempts at thoughtfulness with a sigh and a smile because in the South, everyone knows that "boys will be boys."

A Rabble Rouser *will* treat *you* well, but when you're absent, it's out of sight, out of mind. He is an "in the moment" kind of boy, so whatever is happening is what's on his mind. If you want him to remember where you went on your first date and when you had your first kiss, you'll have to remind him yourself. He might recall the month of your birthday, but the exact date will escape him. And don't get your panties in a wad when he *does* have the memory for the date of the next Ole Miss/State game or who won the last five NASCAR races. It's just his way, and if you're planning on sticking with him for the long term, you'll have to get used to it.

If you are hell-bent on being with a Rabble Rouser, remember one thing: At heart, he is just a twelve-year-old who wants to have fun. That means you will have to take care of him and, if you want anything done, you'll most likely have to do it yourself. While that can be frustrating as hell, you'll have to look at the flip side to put up with him. Life with him will be unpredictable, exciting, and a real joyride.

THE LONE WOLF

The **Lone Wolf** is a guy who is somewhat unattainable, but very attractive in a dangerous sort of way. He is self-absorbed and aloof—a real challenge for some girls. This guy has PMS just like we do. He's intense, and when things are going his way, he'll take you to the moon! But—and there's always a "but" with the Lone Wolf—he's moody. If things don't go his way, he can be pure hell to be around.

My friend Mimi is involved with Beau, a musician in a local band. There is something sort of artsy and mysterious about him. Since she's started dating Beau, Mimi has changed before our very eyes. Why, in the past, she'd never seen the point of poetry because to her, "It's just a bunch of mumbo jumbo and people tryin' to look smart." Suddenly, if Beau wants to go to hear a poetry reading, Mimi wants to go, too. He has a tattoo, so she got one. You should've seen her mama's face when she walked in with a butterfly the size of a dollar sitting right there above her butt! Anyway, a Lone Wolf expects you to do what he does, love what he likes. This is fine with Mimi because she never did have many independent thoughts. Beau is not very sociable and isn't interested in meeting any of Mimi's friends.

A Lone Wolf's mother was absent from his life in one way or the other. She might have been dead, or she might have been so preoccupied with the relationship with her husband that she barely had time for her children. The female in this child's life might have been a stepmother who didn't have the heart or knack for raising a kid. The bond with the major female in his childhood might be described as a "love/hate" kind of thing. He was never exposed to a healthy male/female relationship. Therefore, he had to come up with his own idea of what women are like, what they want, and how they figure into his life.

A word of caution about the Lone Wolf must be offered here. A Lone Wolf is only comfortable in *his* world, on his turf. Even if you manage to attract and snag a Lone Wolf, it may not last long because there's no room for personal growth. If you decide to become a chameleon and take on his interests, you'd better not outdo him because he can't handle the competition. Then, if you want to do something different from what he wants, he will look at your pursuits with disdain and superiority. So as long as you want to stay in the same spot, never really changing, never really growing, this is the man for you.

I am not trying to scare you away from your Lone Wolf if that's what you want. All I'm saying here is that he is conflicted about women, and is likely to treat you according to how he feels that day. So my advice is pretty simple: either lower your expectations or run!

THE MAMA'S BOY

This guy is extremely loyal, and understands the importance of respecting the women in his life. He is a great guy, really, but he comes with some tough, leathery baggage—his mother.

You see, a **Mama's Boy** has been taught by his mama that his "s*&# don't stink." He believes her, and she will never be replaced by another woman in his life. He has grown up accustomed to constant adoration and mothering. He'd be damn near anal about his own life if not for one thing: A Mama's Boy expects his *mother* to show up and do all the cleaning and organizing for him. It's probably not a surprise that his mama has run off many a girl that he liked because, after all, she knew better how to take care of him, how to fix his favorite meal, and how he is the symbol of perfection to which everyone else, when compared, falls short. Perhaps the most dangerous thing about dating a mama's boy is that no matter what, in his mama's eyes, nothing a Mama's Boy does wrong is ever his fault. And that means if you're thinking of having a long-term relationship with him, a lot of the disagreements will be two on one—him and his mama against you!

My good friend Peter is a Mama's Boy who lives over his mama's garage apartment. When he met Anna, she was everything he'd dreamed of, and he told me he thought she was *the one*. "Have you introduced her to your mother yet?" I asked Peter this because I knew what a formidable force she could be. (She only met me once a few years ago and quickly informed him that under no circumstances did I measure up to her adorable boy.) No, he responded, he'd been much too busy. That was code for "Hell, no, 'cause if I did, Anna would be history!" Given the way his mother treated past girlfriends, you can't blame him for being terrified.

A Southern woman knows and accepts the importance of family, especially mothers. She's family and she's been credited for raising this wonderful, if not perfect, man. He gets his validation from his mother, and is not expected to do a thing in their relationship. He truly doesn't get why all of his relationships with women can't be this easy because, after all, he's been taught that the sun rises and sets with him! His mother is totally in control of their relationship, and his end of the bargain is to make a big to-do over her when it counts—her birthday, anniversary, holidays, and so on.

If you are in love with a Mama's Boy, at first you might expect that his mama won't be first place anymore now that you're in the picture. But honey, it just doesn't work that way. A Mama's Boy typically doesn't get that he must accommodate two women in his life, and so he doesn't take the necessary steps to nip any potential trouble in the bud. You will be expected to idolize him just as his mother does. You will always have to compete with Mama, which makes for a terribly difficult situation where no one wins. The best you can hope for is to make points with his mama and one sure way to do it is to let her continue to be number one—or at least let her *think* she is—so that she won't feel threatened.

With that said, although Anna loved her Mama's Boy dearly, it became evident very early on that there were three people in that relationship, and there would continue to be until one of them died. Anna wasn't sure she could stick it out that long. Peter's family had a reputation for living well into their nineties!

So if you are attracted to a Mama's Boy, just know that while he may be crazy about you, it will be crucial that Mama likes you, too, because you'll be spending lots of time together. They say "three's a crowd," but when it comes to a Mama's Boy, it's just the way it is!

THE SERIAL DATER

The **Serial Dater** is one hotbed of competition, but what he's really doing is competing with himself. This guy is never satisfied, moving from one woman to the next. Every woman is a potential challenge for him.

Take Richard, for example. Richard is not really my friend, but more of an acquaintance of mine because he can't really be friends with women—mostly because he always winds up dating them. He thinks he's the expert on women and what they want. What's funny is that he always seems to know the wants and needs of all the women in the world—except for the one he's currently got!

Even though he says he wants to settle down, Richard never seems able to be satisfied with the size of his trophy. Last summer, he was dating Tiffany, the most gorgeous thing you've ever laid eyes on. Her shiny brown hair was perfectly coiffed, and she had legs that went on forever! Richard confirmed that Tiffany was indeed really hot, but was "so dumb she needed instructions to climb a ladder." So he moved on to Linda who was not only beautiful, but also number one in her medical school class. You're thinking that finally it looks as though Richard met his perfect match, right? Oh, no ma'am, that would be too easy. It seems that Richard now wants a woman who has her own money and doesn't need his—now he wants beautiful, smart, and *rich*. Are you getting my point? This is a man who can't be trusted and who perhaps doesn't really know what he wants, despite all his big talk. While women see this sort of man as a challenge, a man they can tame or fix, don't fall into the trap of the Serial Dater! There's a saying my friend Sally used to repeat: "There will always be more silk blouses." The Serial Dater wants someone who is pretty, smart, nice, rich, successful, fit . . . you get the idea. He wants a woman to be all of these things and once he realizes she isn't (because, let's face it, no one is perfect), then he will go lookin' for another silk blouse.

If you're still hell-bent on having him, just remember that you might just be practice for the next "Miss Perfect" he thinks up! So if you're up for it, simply enjoy the ride until *he's* ready for it to be over.

How did the Serial Dater get this way? His mama was all about appearances—mainly her own. She'd spend God knows how much money and time getting herself all dolled up for the country club dance, but didn't care what her child had to wear to his Homecoming Dance. Her life revolved around her social events, not her children. As a boy, the Serial Dater wanted what his friends had. He wanted a mama as pretty as Toby's who went to all of his football games. He wanted a mama as smart as Jack's who always helped with school projects and was probably the reason Jack won the Science Fair every year! He wanted a mama who could cook like Junior's, who always fed all the boys when they went to her house.

So no wonder a Serial Dater always thinks the grass is greener, or there are more "silk blouses." He came up with a fantasy woman based a little on his mama, but a whole lot more on his friends' moms. He truly believes there is a perfect woman out there and will search ad infinitum 'til he finds her.

THE PREP

A close relative of the Mama's Boy is the **Prep**. He is always a part of the herd, but never really the leader. In other words, if everybody else is jumping off into that big, dirty ol' Mississippi River, he'll do it, too, but never first! Appearances matter immensely, and he is consumed by his own. The only reason he is concerned about a woman's appearance is because he sees it as a reflection of his own taste.

My favorite Prep friend is Preston III. But you have to say Preston *the* Third because it sounds so much more pretentious than it ought to that way. You also have to understand that this is generational. His dad has been introducing him as "Preston *the* Third" since he was born. He is a trust fund baby who doesn't have his grandfather's money yet, but knows it'll be his one day. He has been taught that cowshit is cowshit whether it comes with a college degree or not—the only difference is he thinks his smells better!

Preston buys Polo and Izod shirts—he's plumb naked without a logo on his chest—and his loafers are always polished. His khakis are starched with a formidable crease on each leg. He has a neat, nondescript haircut, but displays no individual personal style. He drives the "in" car, and always knows the most high-falutin' restaurant to dine in or the most posh club for dancing. At the country club, Preston *the* Third is barely distinguishable from the others in the pool of Preps having cocktails and steaks. He's not going to stick his neck out and do anything risky or controversial. If he hears something is classy, then that is what he does. At the center of the Prep's world are the country club, his mother and father's social status, and his old fraternity brothers from college. He's a nice guy, but he just ain't got no backbone! He's safe, predictable, and at least you know he won't embarrass you. But rowdy women beware: If you like to have a good time and cause a little trouble now and then, you might find yourself stifled by the Prep's rule-following ways. So if you're serious about dating a prep, you'll need to be on your best behavior!

A Prep has never heard his mama fart or burp. When she was young and single, she was taught to think that social graces are more desirable than, let's say, her skills in the bedroom. She never misses her weekly manicure, pedicure, and facial because what she presents outwardly is paramount over what is on the inside, and she has passed this on to her son. The menus at the fancy restaurants she frequents are far superior to anything she might cook. Who she knows trumps what she knows, any day of the week. Well, you get my point. If you want a Prep, understand this: while he is a perfectly nice, respectable man, he gives little, if none at all, thought to who he is, what he really wants, and whether it's okay to stray from his zone of class and comfort. He just doesn't understand the *need* to be any other way.

THE PRISS

The **Priss** is a third cousin of the Mama's Boy. I know you might immediately think he is gay, but not necessarily. A Southern Priss knows his food, wines, furniture, fabrics, and operas. All of his senses are accentuated. Take clothing, for example. A Prep buys whatever is considered classic. Your Good Ol' Boy wouldn't know cotton from silk, nor would he care. Not Mimi's brother, Niles, though. He can look at a sweater and tell you whether it's 100 percent cashmere or a wool blend. He knows the right wine to serve with veal. He hates wrinkles, so he puts more starch in his shirts than you'd find in a whole field of rice. In fact, Niles hates wrinkles in his life as well. For him, order is everything. Surprises are very annoying and are seen threatening to topple the safe world he has created. He doesn't date much because his standards, in my humble opinion, are way too high. But when Niles does meet his "Miss Right," there's no doubt she'll be as knowledgeable as he is, and just as predictable.

While the Priss claims to be nothing like his mama, he can't help but resemble her. The Priss's dad was probably gone a lot with his work, so Mama did most of the raising, and she wanted her son to have the best. He was taught many things, and was assured there was nothing he couldn't master. The downside of this is that a Priss is not interested in anything or anyone he can't master. So if you find yourself attracted to a Priss, you can't ever let him know that you are more knowledgeable about *anything* than he is, because he won't be able to handle it! You can expect to have a great friendship with a Priss, but there will be little romance or sex. He'll be much more impressed with the thread count of the sheets than what goes on between them!

THE SOUTHERN HEART/YANKEE BRAIN

Next to last, you have your **Southern Heart/Yankee Brain**. This is a man who is dissatisfied with the South. Although he was raised here, he's convinced that the South needs to change and that living elsewhere has *got* to be better: yet he doesn't really want to leave. He is direct, up front, and independent minded. Clothing and other outward appearances don't matter to him because he doesn't care what others think about him. Henry is my best example. He reminds me of one of those 1961 Southern Kennedy democrats. He is liberal in his opinions and politics, and progressive about what he'd like to see changed. I love Henry on 'count of he's the real deal. Down here though, his forwardness and openness make Southerners uncomfortable. Southerners would rather "talk around" something instead of going directly at it. Down South, there's something unsettling about being a "what-you-see-is-what-you-get" guy. That's unfortunate for a lot of folks, because Henry has a strong sense of responsibility, of what's right and wrong, and of what makes life meaningful. If you date him, you'd better be as comfortable in your skin as he is in his own since he doesn't suffer fools. If you are lucky enough to be called his friend, he will always be loyal and true. That doesn't sound so bad to me, does it to you?

A Southern Heart/Yankee Brain's mom takes no crap off of anyone. She was the mom who pissed off the other mothers after she was the first to give the household help a raise. She figured if it was okay in her mind, then it *was* okay, and she didn't need anyone's permission or approval. She is wise and practical, and a real firebrand when she makes up her mind. Her influence on her son is tremendous. She understands him as a man, and fosters his self-reliance. This guy has a very close relationship with his mom, and he can talk to her about anything—even the gory details of a date, if she asks. He is intolerant of clingy, smothering people and refuses to go along with the crowd.

When you are involved with a Southern Heart/Yankee Brain, you'd better be independent and not afraid to show it. Being with him might not always make you popular, since some of his conversations or opinions will probably make people uncomfortable. He won't sit still if you are wallowing in self-pity—he'll expect you to get up, put your big-girl panties on and deal with it!

THE SOUTHERN GENTLEMAN

Last, we've got the **Southern Gentleman**, the epitome of grace. He's comfortable in both a man and woman's world, and he is confident in just about every situation. He doesn't have to be perfect, but he's sure to be able to handle whatever you dish out. He is not intimidated by strong women because, deep down, he really doesn't believe that they are. A woman might be strong in the boardroom, but he knows she is just as likely to go home and drown her stress in a half-gallon of chocolate chip ice cream and the Lifetime channel.

Claire is married to a Southern Gentleman. Jim is well mannered, but masculine. He's a good listener, an eager learner, and a kind person. He knows to walk behind a lady when going up the stairs and in front of her going down in case she falls. Because he has an infinite amount of respect and appreciation for them, he puts the women in his life on a pedestal. He is protective of them, but not possessive. Jim loves to cook dinner for Claire and me, and is completely at ease with being the only guy in the room. He also likes to get up early to go hunting. He's as comfortable riding in a Porsche as he is a pickup truck, and probably knows the inner workings of both. He loves to have a good time, but knows how to be responsible. Jim is loyal to his family and is crazy about his friends. I guess the best way to sum up a Southern Gentleman's relationship with a woman is this: he doesn't need you in a dependent, clingy way—instead, he *wants* you.

A Southern Gentleman's relationship with his mama is fluid so as to meet her needs. The approach is one of give-and-take, and he is well aware that she is the matriarch of the family. Regardless of his age, he treats her well. As a teenager, he is respectful; in his twenties, he is kind and helpful; in his thirties, he begins to be more of an equal once he has children of his own. He can talk to her about many things, but also knows there are certain topics that are taboo. He wants to please her, but will not sell his soul to do it. He will not expect you to do it, either, so there is the possibility that you can have a comfortable, easy, and perhaps even close relationship with her. But he *is* looking for the same great qualities in a woman that he values in himself. If this is the kind of man you want, know that life with a Southern Gentleman will be better than fat-free chocolate!

Just so you know it, there are no purebreds of these categories. The various concoctions are endless. You can have a mixture of a Redneck and a Rabble Rouser. A Yankee/Midwestern Wannabe and a Southern Gentleman. Or maybe a Serial Dater, Mama's Boy, with a bit of Lone Wolf thrown in. You get the picture, right? These categories are a starting point, and you might want to add some of your own. But remember, no man will ever fit neatly into just one package. If you want a certain type of man in your life, it's up to you to figure out how to get the one you want, bless your little heart!

Top 5 Things a Southern Belle Never Wants to See in a Man

1   Nose and ear hair

2   Missing teeth

3   Toe jam

4   Skidmarks in his underwear

5   _____

(fill in this blank yourself!)

CHAPTER THREE

Picture Yourself as a Southern Belle

The biggest myth about Southern women is that we are frail types—fainting on our sofas . . . Nobody where I grew up ever acted like that. We were about as fragile as coal trucks.

—Lee Smith

When preparing to nab yourself a man in Southern-belle style, you not only need to know about the types of men that are out there, you also have to know about the Southern belle personality. After canvassing many a Southern lady for their opinions and input, I've come up with four really strong types of Southern female personalities. Now you might be asking yourself if there are only four types because Southern belles are just that simple. My heavenly days! There are plenty of distinctive Southern women out there, but I had to narrow it down somehow. Plus, do you really want to spend your time reading a book about women? We're here to get you a man, so I'm fixin' to offer up a little twelve-question quiz here to figure out the belle with whom you most identify. Please don't go off with your pistol half-cocked and sneak a peek at the answers! And another thing, in case you haven't got the sense God gave a monkey, remember this quiz is supposed to be fun, so keep your mind open and have a good time with it.

Circle the letter beside the answer that sounds most like you.

1. *What's your favorite pastime?*

    a. Shopping, gossip, and looking at myself in the mirror

    b. Reading and listening to/attending the opera

    c. Taking a class or learning a new skill

    d. Baking cookies for the needy

2. *What techniques do you use to get a man to notice you?*

    a. All I have to do is walk into the room.

    b. I make him feel he's the most interesting man in the room.

    c. I try to engage in a lively discussion about our jobs, common interests, etc.

    d. I wait for him to notice me or I send a friend over to "test the waters."

3. *Describe your perfect date.*

    a. Dinner, champagne, and of course, a gift

    b. Picnic, wine, and a romantic walk

    c. Meeting at the local bar to drink, party, and dance

    d. A movie and popcorn, and maybe ice cream afterward

4. *If you were going camping with your man, what would you take along?*

    a. Hotel reservations, my eye mask, and a scented candle

    b. A portable coffeemaker—I don't want to suffer.

    c. My iPod, Blackberry, and sleeping pills

    d. A good, warm sleeping bag, sensible shoes, and a map

5. *What's in your purse?*

   a. Hairspray, makeup and mirror, and credit cards (not necessarily my own)
   b. Lipstick, breath mints, and an emergency twenty
   c. My day planner, cell phone, and business card holder
   d. First-aid kit, a pen and paper, and a scrunchy

6. *What did your mama teach you about men?*

   a. It's just as easy to love a rich one as a poor one.
   b. Character and class make the man.
   c. Anything he can do, I can do better.
   d. The right man will take care of me, and my job is to make him happy.

7. *In times of stress, what puts you at ease?*

   a. Booze and my friend's valium
   b. A long, hot bubble bath and a glass of good wine
   c. A long, hard run
   d. Prayer and family

8. *What's your signature dish that you like to prepare for your man?*

   a. A four-course French meal prepared by someone else, but I fib a little and say I cooked it
   b. Handmade yeast rolls and a glazed ham, both of which were my grandmother's recipes
   c. Reservations to his favorite restaurant, or take-out
   d. Whatever he likes

9. *What's the most important thing you learned from watching your mama?*

    a. Appearances are everything—never, ever, never leave the house without "your face on."

    b. Perfect manners and etiquette will take you further than anything in life.

    c. Not to be my mama!

    d. Cooking makes everyone feel loved.

10. *How would you handle a friend who tries to steal your man?*

    a. Tell everyone at the club that she's a backstabbing hussy who should never be trusted.

    b. Hold my head up high because my man would never fall for that piece of trash.

    c. Move on and let her have him—there are plenty of fish in the sea.

    d. A true friend wouldn't do that.

11. *How soon should you have sex with someone you are seeing?*

    a. After I see the the ring.

    b. A lady never tells!

    c. As soon as my schedule allows.

    d. I will only have sex with my husband.

12. *What's your idea of the perfect wedding?*

    a. Twelve bridesmaids, taffeta dresses, big flowers, a poufy white wedding gown, and lots of presents

    b. A classy affair, and a Vera Wang gown

c. Elope—to Vegas or somewhere warm

d. A big family celebration, my mama's wedding dress, and no alcohol

Alrighty then, are you ready to score your answers? If you don't have a majority of answers in one category, don't worry. It just means you are an even more complex woman than this quiz indicates!

Mostly a's: If you answered mostly a's, you are what I like to think of as a Scarlett O'Hara (*Gone With the Wind*) or Suzanne Sugarbaker (*Designing Women*) character. "High Maintenance" might be your middle name. Like Scarlett and Suzanne, you have needs—mostly related to your appearance, but needs nonetheless. You *never* leave the house without makeup and your attire perfectly planned. You have a standing appointment at your favorite beauty parlor to get your hair, nails, and footsies done. In the words of Suzanne, you're the one who will get pulled over by the police "because all of the mirrors in my Mercedes were turned so I could see myself."

While you have a few friends whom you trust, you are usually wary of other people and think they want something from you. If you had been in beauty pageants, you'd have swept every category but one—congeniality. You have your ways of getting what you want, and you do it so well that your target doesn't know what hit him when it's all over. You are industrious and in charge, and you are never without a plan. Your exploits are designed to get what you want while deftly managing to ignore the carnage you leave behind. You have the tendency to be a bit on the melodramatic side—well, really, you are the quintessential drama queen! You love a good calamity and usually you are in the center of it. You are famous for a bitchiness that started pretty much from the time you were in a crib. Your daddy spoiled you rotten and you expect the same treatment from all men.

Nothing in your closet is over six months old because you'd never be caught dead in an outfit worn more than twice. You are the girl who not only dressed beautifully for the prom, but also got all decked out just for final exams. When you started dating, your mama taught you to always keep a man waiting. So if your date is at seven o'clock, you'll be the one still shopping for the perfect pair of shoes at six thirty. You truly don't believe that tardiness is a problem: seven means anywhere from seven to seven thirty. In other words, you're "not late 'til it's almost eight!"

What makes you special is that you expect the best to come to you. You have extremely high expectations and thus you do not believe there is such a thing as "second place." You know that the man who is truly able to capture your heart will love your devious, cunning ways, and would never wish to change you. That's a good thing, too, because he couldn't change you if he wanted to!

Scooter was everything a Scarlett should be. She got her first pedicure and manicure at the age of six. She only had to raise her voice just a tiny bit to get exactly what she wanted. If her parents were intimidated by her manipulating, dramatic ways, they didn't show it. Her every whim was indulged. Her first public appearance was on her uncle's local furniture store commercial, where she proudly proclaimed, "I only sleep in beds from Uncle John's store." (Of course, this was a false prediction, 'cause by the time she grew up, she'd found herself in a whole lot more beds than that!) Her television debut led to her entry in the Tomato Festival Pageant, where she was easily crowned queen. She won the Miss Boll Weevil Beauty Pageant when she was twelve. Her mama thought Scooter had a wonderful future ahead of her, but, by then, Scooter had discovered boys, and they became the new trophies she competed for.

Not long ago, I had a reunion with four friends from All Saints High School. We met at Magnolia's, a fancy-pants restaurant in the heart of town. Scooter was late, of course, but slid into her seat, squealing and caterwauling about how "goooood" it was to see us. She had married the high school quarterback (I thought that only happened in books and movies!), Ted, and he was the president of a bank in Jackson, Mississippi. She was in town visiting her mama and daddy. She showed me what seemed like thousands of pictures of the twins, Alexander (named after Daddy, naturally!) and Catherine, named after her mama. They weren't dressed alike, but, I kid you not, there wasn't a single photo where they weren't color-coordinated right down to their shoes and sandals. When anyone tried to change the subject to talk about themselves, she did a very poor job of pretending to be interested. So we gave in and returned to her favorite topic—Scooter. It turns out that Scooter hadn't changed a bit, and, in her case, I wasn't surprised. Scooter still believes the world revolves around her and assumes the rest of us aren't revolving around her star because we don't know how. She can't fathom why we wouldn't want to be just like her.

In the end, though, you can't help but love a girl like Scooter. She is what she is, and she doesn't pretend to be anything else. She knows she is wonderful, and is pretty sure everyone else knows it.

Mostly b's: If you answered mostly b's, you are more like Julia Sugarbaker, Suzanne's sister. Even though you are also a high-maintenance gal, your attention to yourself is purely obligatory. You keep yourself up because that is what Southern belles have been taught to do, but you're as comfortable in jeans with your hair in a pony tail, as you are wearing a cocktail dress and your hair in an up-do. You like feeling pretty, but you just don't get the emphasis on makeup, hair, and nails.

You are a true lady—or like we say down here, you "act like you've got some raisin'." You are well bred, poised, and polished. Unlike the Scarlett/Suzanne type, you are polite and kind, and other people's feelings are put before your own. When you win at tennis or cards, you downplay your victory and make the others feel good about losing. Other women enjoy your company because you are not intimidating. You would never go out with a redneck or someone below your "station," but you will always be gracious and welcoming toward him. You are a lover of tradition and cherish your family. Just because you are ladylike, don't think you can't take care of yourself.

Liza was someone I wanted to be in high school. Everything

seemed to come easily to her, but she was so nice about it, you couldn't resent her for it. She was captain of the tennis team, president of the debate club, and won the coveted title of Miss Congeniality for our senior yearbook. (You should've seen Scooter—she was not happy about that!) She was good hearted and considerate toward Maggie Littlejohn, the girl with bad skin and horrid BO. She grew up with Hunter Bailey, a sort of boy-version of herself. Her parents and Bailey's were best friends, so it was no big surprise that she married him. (That's another thing I thought happened only on TV or in books!)

At that reunion luncheon with my All Saints friends, Liza was the same size she'd been since high school, despite having given birth to three kids. It appeared that things still came easily to her. She and Bailey were living happily ever after. They still celebrated Christmas with both sets of parents, just as they'd done throughout their childhoods. Her three children were doing fine, but she had to admit that she always looked forward to her regular "girls-only" trips to the Gulf Coast so she could have a break.

Liza was on the board of several organizations in Atlanta and had just won the country club's tennis tournament. As usual, she reported this with no pride or arrogance. She wanted to hear about the rest of us, which was pretty hard to do since Scooter was demanding all the attention. We all agreed that Liza was just damn lucky and we couldn't help but be happy for her.

Mostly c's: Those of you who scored mostly c's fall into a category that was hard to relate to a fictitious character. You're what we call the progressive belle. Think Melanie from *Sweet Home Alabama* or Brenda, who stars in the TV show *The Closer*.

You are ambitious about making a mark in the world, and while you'd love to be in a relationship, getting a man is not on the top of your list of goals. You are equally at ease in a boardroom and on the golf course. Your cell phone is never far from your side. You are so adept at your job that in the time it takes to order fries in the drive-through at McDonald's, you can close a million-dollar deal before the cashier hands you the change. On a date, you will intentionally tell a man you are going to be receiving an important call just so he'll understand from the get-go that he is *not* your priority. And while you prize your independence and self-reliance, it can be intimidating to a lot of men. They think you don't need them (which *is* true), but you *do* enjoy them! If you are a progressive belle, remember: it's okay to show your appreciation for your man without sounding too desperate.

You love to have fun, but you make it clear to everyone around you that you're very much in charge of your own life. That said, you are not above using your charm to get what you want. If you watch *The Closer*, you know what I mean. Behind Brenda's buttery "thaaaank yew" lies a tough, take-no-prisoners attitude that gets results.

You are practical, organized, and realistic. Other kinds of Southern belles will tell you that you are unromantic or unsentimental, but this is most certainly not the case! Your mama and daddy taught you that you're just as good as any ol' man. You have been encouraged to do something more with your life than only to marry and have children. There will be plenty of time for romance and a family later, you believe. So, for now, men are not your focus, but merely supplements to your very busy life. Men are fun to have dinner with, to have sex with, to do many things with— you just don't want any attachments at this point. You have lost many potential keepers and have let a lot of great men slip through the net just because it wasn't the right timing for you. But you are confident that there will be plenty of fish left in the sea.

Martha, a.k.a. TeePee, was fifteen minutes late to our reunion luncheon and arrived with her cell phone practically glued to her ear. Let me explain her nickname. Martha was the first of us to celebrate the rites of passage into womanhood—she got her period first, she shaved first, and she developed breasts first. We were so fascinated by her breasts, especially her nipples. In a fit of giggles one day in the locker room after a grueling game of kickball, Scooter exclaimed that Martha's nipples looked like the Indian teepees we had studied about in school. Thus her name TeePee. Okay, back to lunch. Someone finally had to take TeePee's phone away so we could talk to her.

TeePee had risen quickly in Staffing Logistics, a worldwide corporate headhunting operation. She traveled all over the world and had become the organization's youngest headhunter, evidently a real coup in her line of work. Eventually, the conversation turned to men and children. TeePee asked Scooter about her life and listened quietly as Scooter bragged about her latest tennis trophy and the ball she was hosting at the country club. TeePee asked Scooter if her life was really that perfect. Scooter replied, "Of course! I mean, who wouldn't want my life?" TeePee responded with, "Well, I wouldn't—it sounds a bit self-absorbed. Don't you get sick of everything being the same?" Well, Scooter glanced at the rest of us, rolled her eyes, and shrugged her shoulders. Liza tried to step in and defend Scooter, but TeePee wasn't buying it. It was clear to Scooter and Liza that poor, lonely ambitious TeePee didn't get it.

You see, the progressive belle, like TeePee, loves her friends, but her approach to life is definitely different. It's not that she looks down on her friends—it's just that their lives are so foreign to her. While she will be fiercely loyal to her friends, she's convinced that her life is much more exciting and challenging. When it comes to men, she is sure that the right one will come along and when she's ready, she'll grab hold of him!

Mostly d's: If you answered mostly d's, you might recognize yourself in the characters of Charlene from *Designing Women* or Shelby in *Steel Magnolias*. Although some will tell you you ain't got a grain of sense, that is completely false. You have a sweet, naive wisdom about you that makes you see only the good in others. You are not demanding and are happy to be just where you are in your life. You are a good friend and are never judgmental. You have the best oatmeal cookie recipe, and if a friend is in a pinch, you've been known to help her cook an entire meal for company that's coming.

Your mama taught you that the proverbial white knight does indeed exist, and it is a Southern belle's destiny to be rescued by him. The white knight might be rich or he might be poor, but his aim in life is to take a wife, have a family, and cherish them forever. You are only too happy to oblige him, and you look forward to a life of kids, PTA meetings, church bake sales, and supporting your husband. You know that without your management of the home, your husband could not focus on earning a living. When asked, you never say you are *just* a homemaker. You recognize that this is probably the most important job of all, and you are proud of your contributions. You believe everything will be just fine if you have faith. Your contentment comes from knowing your husband and children are happy. But keep in mind, you are not as meek as some might think. You might not put it to use often, but you possess a quiet strength. If someone dares to mess with your family, you will become a lioness in a New York minute!

My fourth classmate at the luncheon was Loreen, who is your classic Charlene or Shelby. She married Josh, a man who works for her daddy. They have a litter of kids, okay, only four—but it seems like a litter to me! Josh, Loreen, and the kids do everything together as a family. In fact, Loreen was shocked when she heard Liza talking about vacations away from her kids! Although they could use some extra income, she doesn't have a job. Loreen is the organizer for the church bake sale, and her homemade chocolate chip cookies are legendary! She is the secretary for the PTA and is willing to volunteer for just about any job the school needs. She loves to cook for big crowds, and she tries to have the neighbors and their kids over for a cookout at least once a month. All of the kids on her block play at her house after school because she is the "fun" mom (the endless supply of chocolate chip cookies doesn't hurt either!), so she is only too happy to accommodate them. Keeping her marriage alive and exciting is very important to her, so she and Josh have a standing date once a week.

During our discussions about our lives and amid some of the comments made about our choices, Loreen said she couldn't imagine her life without Josh and the kids. Then she quietly expressed to TeePee that she worried about the fact that her career was not going to keep her warm at night. She wasn't rude, mind you, and TeePee seemed to take it well. TeePee lovingly remarked that perhaps Loreen knows nothing about the big, bad world, and didn't have a clue about how great her own life is. Despite our differences, we managed to have a lovely lunch, after which I went straight home and fixed myself a big ol' gin and tonic!

No matter what their personality type, all Southern belles want to think that their life is the best, the most enviable one. Southern belles can be chameleons, able to transform from one type to another depending on where they want to blend in or who they are with. I am not saying they are frauds—it's just that they have the ability to wake up in a new world every day if they so choose— sort of like a goose.

Take my friends Kate and Alice. Kate is the sweetest thing you have ever known. She has eight perfect-attendance pins from her Sunday School class and wouldn't say "bullshit" even if it were the main ingredient in her mama's potato salad recipe! Kate is not a risk taker or a rule breaker.

Alice, on the other hand, hardly ever darkens the church doors. Why, the last time anyone saw her in church was at her daddy's funeral, and the preacher had to tell her where to find the bathroom. Anyway, last year, Kate and Alice each took the most unique and out-of-character vacations.

Kate went to the beach. That's not unusual for us Southerners, but she went *alone*! Upon her return, I picked up her digital camera while I waited for her to get her luggage. I was scanning through her pictures when, lo and behold, there she was smack dab on a nude beach. Yep, you heard me correctly—a nude beach, not just a topless beach, which would have been scandalous enough. She was proudly sitting on a chaise lounge, nekkid as a billy goat, surrounded by several Corona bottles and a herd of fully tanned men who had obviously been helping her drink them. Kate's still mad at me for going through the pictures. She swore me to secrecy. But I'm never one to pass up a good story! Sorry, Kate.

Now the same summer, Alice left on her vacation but sort of disappeared. For two weeks, no one could reach her. When she got back she wouldn't say where she'd been. Of course, rehab had to be the obvious answer, but while she drank and liked to have fun, she had never let it get out of hand. And drugs didn't seem likely since that's what killed her daddy, and she was always the first to leave a party if drugs came out. So, by now, you have probably come to the same conclusion that we had—boob job. Nope, hers were damn near perfect, the bitch, and all of her other parts really didn't need any work. She did have ugly little toes, but no one gets those fixed.

It was a true mystery, and we were all a little ashamed of our speculations and afraid of what the truth might be. But the truth *does* prevail, and one Saturday night not long after Alice returned from her trip, I ran into her at an Italian restaurant. She introduced me to her date, Frankie. He was in from New Jersey of all places, visiting her for the weekend. Now I was about to explode with curiosity so I invited myself for a quick drink, certain there was more to this story than met the eye.

Frankie had sort of a commanding presence about him. He was nice looking, and while he seemed a little quiet, it was that kind of quiet that makes you want to be damn sure you're there when he finally decides to speak. My patience paid off. I managed to squeeze out the tidbit that they had met while on vacation in— are you ready?—Central America! Finally, the mystery was solved. Alice must have been on some hedonistic, wild adventure in an exotic Central American resort. Imagine my surprise (okay, disappointment, really) when the resort turned out to be a small village in Nicaragua. They were on a trip sponsored by UNICEF to rebuild a children's clinic that had burned to the ground. Oddly enough, Alice swore me to secrecy, too. Oh, well . . .

You get my point, right? We Southern belles get what we want and do whatever we have to do to get it. Whatever personality type you might be, you are now well on the road to figuring out what kind of man you want. The great thing about finding a man is that there are plenty of them just waiting to be dazzled by your charm and special style. You don't have to try and be a different personality, just be yourself—there's a man out there meant just for you! So ladies, let's get down to the business of huntin', shall we?

Top 5 Things a Southern Belle Always Has in Her Purse

1. Cell phone (in case she loses her charge card)
2. Charge card (in case she loses her cell phone)
3. Breath mints
4. Keys to Mama and Daddy's house
5. Condoms (tucked discreetly in the side zipper pocket!)

CHAPTER FOUR

Flirting

Or, Emulate His Dog—Be Fetching, but Don't Beg!

Even Southern babies know that "Gimme some sugar" is not a request for the white, granular sweet substance that sits in a pretty little bowl in the middle of the table.

—Anonymous

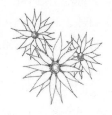

We may not have been born with it, but ever since a Southern belle was knee-high to a grasshopper, we have been flirting. First, we honed our skills on our daddies. Once we got him wrapped around our dainty little fingers, we realized that we had a power that is mightier than y'all have ever seen. Flirting is just what we *do*.

Merriam-Webster defines flirting as "to show superficial or casual interest or liking; to behave amorously without serious intent." I take issue with that description. Flirting, in the South, is not meant to be fake or insincere. Southern belles are charmers, and flirting is seen as our God-given right to use our feminine wiles to attract attention. In fact, we flirt with just about everybody, male and female. In the South, a lack of flirting is as serious as Sunday brunch without a Bloody Mary! And everyone down here knows you simply *cannot* host or attend a brunch on a Sunday morning without a yummy Bloody Mary in your hand! Now, there are a ton of so-called experts out there who want to tell you all about flirting. They'll tell you what to do and what to say and what to wear and how to act. And I'm tellin' you that you don't need any of their fancy advice. Keep this little book right close to your side because this is all the advice you'll ever need.

Think of flirting like fishin'. If you want to catch something, you have to send a retractable sign that you're interested. Flirting is merely putting on the right lure to catch the kind of fish you want. Sometimes you'll catch a fish, and throw it back immediately. Or you'll fight to get the fish into your boat, only to throw it back later. Other times, you'll like the fish you caught, but you just can't decide if it's the keeper. Or you'll be about to catch a fish and you let it get away. And then sometimes, you'll catch *the* one you want to mount on your wall—the prize fish!

I've done my share of flirting and so have my girlfriends. I've broken down the system to eight steps.

1. *The Glimpse*—When you spot a guy you want to meet, look in his direction. Keep doing this until your eyes meet his, but only for a split second. Then look away and make some gesture that signifies you're a bit embarrassed that he caught you looking. Men are simple creatures. It doesn't take much work to boost their egos! Just an itsy, bitsy glance of the eye can make him weak in the knees.

2. *The Moves*—If you are successful and you get "the glimpse" mastered and he has seen you, be prepared to make the first move, but don't act all obvious about it. Men can be shy about flirting, so you need to show you're not afraid to make

the first move. I don't mean you have to get all Sharon Stone in *Basic Instinct* with the guy—what you wanna do here is tease a man with just a little skin. You might draw your skirt up just a bit so he can take a gander at your glorious gams. Or perhaps you could lean forward ever so slightly as to give him a peek at your sexy cleavage. (If you are cleavage-challenged, you might have to bend all the way over and pretend to adjust your shoe!) You can tilt your head or gingerly scratch your neck. Anything that is provocative is good here, but don't show too much. We are not giving it away for free here!

3. *The Two-Drink Rule*—My friend Lulu taught me this. When you're out to flirt and possibly meet a man, you don't want to be sloshed while you're doing it. I've seen many a woman who thinks she's adorable after downing a couple of glasses of wine, a few beers, and a shot of tequila. Yes, it probably makes you feel less inhibited, but that's also the problem. This is not the time to be wild as a March hare unless you want to be known as "that drunk girl over there making a sorry ass out of herself." If this is the case, drink on. But according to Lulu, you should make two drinks last the whole night in case you wind up seeing someone worthy of your time and on whom you'd like to make a favorable impression.

4. *Pretty Is as Pretty Does*—You are as pretty as the effort you put into it. This is not, and I repeat, not the time to wear your eighteen-hour bra with those straps wide as the road cut-

ting off your circulation. Nor is it the time to wear what we politely refer to down here as your "granny panties"—those big, white, cotton underpants that come up to your breasts. Dress for a bit of visual access—no turtlenecks, scarves, etc. Remember, pretty is as pretty does. You don't necessarily need to show off your lingerie while flirting unless you really want to, but when you have on your sexy underwear, your inner princess comes out and gives you that extra boost of confidence to get the job done.

5. *The Sting*—Here comes the most challenging part for most girls. We're moving in on our target here and we are gonna have to come up with something to say that doesn't sound completely absurd or just plain stupid. What you're trying to do is make contact in a nonthreatening manner. And let's face it, the best way to do that is to butter up his ego. Here are some safe, flirty remarks you can say to open the conversation.

❀ "Does it seem hot in here to you?"
❀ "I do declare, you look like you could use a drink."
❀ "I hope you don't mind my saying so, but you have the nicest smile."
❀ "Have my eyes deceived me or are you the most handsome man in this room?"
❀ "You're so cute, I could eat you up with a spoon."

❀ "I'd say hello, but my mama always told me to stay away from boys like you."

❀ "Well, I don't know what it is, but I just feel like I already know you."

6. *The Play*—If the sting was successful, you are ready to hold his attention long enough to determine whether or not he's a loser. This is done pretty simply. Men love to talk about themselves, so ask questions. The more open-ended they are, the better. For example, don't ask, "What do you do for a living?" Instead, try, "Tell me about your work." Pay attention to what he's saying because his words will offer up invaluable insight into what makes him tick. Small compliments work well here. Try, "Why I just love your shirt. The color looks great on you," or something even more to the point like, "Great tie!"

7. *The Touch*—This may sound a little tricky, but it's not. When you are interested in someone, touching can be quite effective. No, I'm not talking about feeling him up. A playful hit to his shoulder when you laugh will make him feel that his joke was funnier than it actually was. If you're discussing a more serious topic, a gentle pat on his forearm is a good move. If you are really interested in him and have the nerve, perhaps you can pretend he has something on the corner of his mouth and slightly wipe it with your napkin. This works well unless there is actually something on his mouth and it's just plain gross—try something else in that case. Touch is a way of letting people into your space and entering theirs without being too forward. It will let a man know you are open to his attentions.

8. *The Qualifier*—So you've made it to step 8 and it's time to throw him back in the pond or keep him as a potential catch. Now what? It's easy, really. If you are not interested, there are several things you can try. You can keep looking at your watch or around the room. This is the signal that tells him "you aren't it and you need to go away." If he is smart enough, he oughta get this pretty quickly. Or tell him he reminds you of your last boyfriend that you had to take a restraining order out on because he was such a creep. If he's three pickles shy of a quart, just say "nice talking to ya" and walk away. Most people understand that level of rejection.

Now if you want to keep him, be subtle. You will have to find a delicate way of giving him the opportunity to ask for your number or a date. For example, casually mention that you are working only half a day tomorrow (or a few days from now) and then you are going shopping. You might even just order a pizza and rent a movie so you can hang out at home. This doesn't make you sound desperate, but lets him know you aren't doing anything *that* important. If he gets it and asks for your number, a true Southern belle acts pleasantly surprised and then hands it over. Again, there are some men who're so dumb, they could throw themselves on the ground and miss. With them, you may have to be more direct.

Stroke his ego a little. Tell him he "sure is nice" (that's a very long, hard *I* in nice) and that it'd be great to talk to him some more, but you have to go. This should get his attention. Don't let him fool you into asking him out. If he's interested, and you have done your job well, he *will* pursue you. He likes to believe he's in charge and why should we ruin his fun? Be patient, be your delightful self, and a qualifier is sure to step up to the plate.

DANGER ZONES

So what if you made a mistake and this is not someone you want to talk to? As Mama said, if you can't say something nice, then just shut the hell up. Men aren't real smart when it comes to reading the sign over your head that is silently saying, "Please go away before I stick myself in the eye with my finger because you are the most boring, dull human being on the face of the planet!" They seem to start sweatin' when the conversation stalls, and your silence may be just what it takes to send him running back to the guys at the other end of the room!

On the other hand, sometimes knowing how to gracefully get rid of a guy is just as important as knowing how to gracefully get a guy! So if your silence is not being "heard," you can politely excuse yourself to go to the powder room, or say, "Excuse me, I think I see someone I know." You can even say, "It was so nice talking to you," before you turn and walk away.

Feel free to flirt with anyone you choose, but I feel an obligation to warn you about a few danger zones when it comes to flirting. No man is totally off-limits, but you might want to approach some with a little extra caution. If you run into any of the situations below, you'd do well to run in the opposite direction.

If He's Drunker Than Hell

If the guy you are flirting with is drunker than a skunk, it's only common sense to avoid him, especially if he's yelling things like, "Hey, honey come over here and let me take you down South!"

Trust me, honey, this guy is certainly not worth your trouble because he probably won't even remember your name tomorrow. Let him make a stupid ass of himself if he wants to, but don't waste your precious time trying to get anything noteworthy out of his mouth!

If He's Married

No matter how cute, charming, or funny he is, always remember this rule of thumb: Look at his ring finger first! If there's a ring on it, run. If there's a distinct white stripe where his ring used to be because he took it off to pick up women, run. Trust me, it will save you a lot of heartache later, that's for sure.

A married man might be a heap of fun to flirt with, but he still has a wife, y'all! If you don't speak "married," here's a quick starter course for you:

If he says: "I guess I should tell you I'm married."
Then he means: "I'm looking for hanky-panky."

If he says: "Well, things aren't so great at home."

Then he means: "I'm bored and maybe you can help me spice up my life!"

If he says: "We're in the process of a divorce."

Then he means: "She doesn't know it yet, and it may not even happen, but don't you feel sorry for me?"

If he says: I know you think I'm making this up, but my wife *really doesn't* understand me."

Then he means: "I can't get my way every time I pout anymore."

If he says: "We're just different, that's all."

Then he means: "She's faithful, I'm not."

If he says: "We have an agreement about our relationship and she doesn't care what I do."

Then he means: "I'm full of s#@*!"

Blah, blah, blah. Don't squander your time on someone who might be fun temporarily, but for whom you'll have to compete for his attentions later. Hell's bells, girl, you *can* do better!

If He's Got a Girlfriend

If you're flirting with a guy whose girlfriend is in the room, that's just downright wrong! Southern belles would *never* humiliate another woman like that and they certainly don't have to stoop that low. On the flip side, if he's flirting with you and she's around, understand that if he's that disrespectful of her, he'll do the same to you. That dog just won't hunt, and you should have no part in it.

You might be wonderin' what you should do if you're already flirting with a man and he accidentally lets it slip that he has a girlfriend. First, don't be afraid to put him on the spot. Respond with something like, "Oh, you've got a girlfriend? Where is *she* tonight?" That lets him know you heard what he said and he is being put on the spot. Second, it's still okay to flirt, but don't look at this guy as a potential keeper. He's still disrespectin' his girl!

If He's Gay

A lot of women in the South are drawn to sensitive, well-dressed men, and if you've ever believed that you could be so fetching and tantalizing that you could "straighten" a guy out— well, honey, you wouldn't be the first! But the bottom line is, if he's gay, you shouldn't go there. No, no, and no. You are much better off keeping him as a friend-friend. It will hurt a lot less and be much more fun!

If He's Your Friend's Date

This one might be a little difficult to navigate. Is it appropriate to flirt with a friend's date if she's not serious about him?

For Whom the Belle Tolls

A fair and highly scientific* survey of ten Southern belles on the subject of flirting with a friend's date yielded the following results:

1 Three out of ten Southern belles agree that all's fair in love and war.

2 Six out of ten Southern belles agree that they'd "flat tear her up and be all over her like white on rice if she did that to me."

3 One Southern belle agrees that "no real lady would ever entertain that notion—that would make her lower than a snake's belly."

So is it worth it to flirt with a friend's date? You'll just have to decide that for yourself, but I never met a man that was so darn enthralling that it was worth it to lose one of my girlfriends.

*The rum and cokes were the "scientific" part,

THE BELLE'S GUIDE TO HUNTIN' AND FISHIN'

You remember how we classified men back in chapter 2? Well, where are you gonna meet them? Well, depending on which type of man you'd like to meet, there are a wide variety of places to get started. While these locales are not exclusive to a particular group, I do promise that if you go to these places, you will be successful. Here are a few of our favorites:

The Redneck

Where to find him: Your best shot at finding a Redneck is at any outdoor activity where there's lots of mud, food, and beer, from outdoor music festivals to tractor pulls to the state fair. You might also find him at a car show, or more accurately, at a truck show. He'll be real knowledgeable about the engines, speed range, and the size of its bed.

The approach: If you wanna attract this guy, you have to be one with his world. You have to enjoy, or learn to enjoy activities that are solely "his"—from drinking beer to attending a good motorcycle race. You don't have to act like a smarty-pants about it, but if you possess special knowledge about cars, trucks, and the like, find a way to weave it into the conversation. Try, "Have you seen that new Ford F-250? Man, that baby sure has some power and a great ride!" If you have the opportunity, you can always provocatively lean over his motorcycle or the hood as you inspect his "engine." If you really want this guy, never, ever make a comment about how he's dressed. When it comes to the Redneck, you have to take him as he is—or not take him at all!

The Good Ol' Boy

Where to find him: The Mossy Oak store is probably the very best place to meet the Good Ol' Boy. This is mecca for him! But if you're looking for a different type of venue, try lookin' at church on Sunday—he'll most likely be there with his mama and daddy. But this in no way suggests that he is a straitlaced, no-fun kind of guy. He simply loves his mama, and is a good son, which means he wants to please her. The third place you might find him is at his niece's ball game. If you'll remember, he's a loyal sort, and loves his family.

The approach: If you plan on flirtin' at Mossy Oak, you'd better know something about sports. This can be a bit tricky here because Mossy Oak caters to the big outdoorsman and there is a lot to know. My advice is to play dumb and let him teach you. For example, if you happen to be in the fishin' section and there's a particularly cute fella checking out the gear, try this: "I'm thinking of buying a new fishing pole. What size is yours?" See? You get to flirt and he gets to feel like the sports pro he fancies himself to be.

Now at church, you'll have to be careful about how you flirt here because you don't wanna look like a hussy. Try offering him a hymnal to share or asking him the way to the Sunday school class.

The ballgame is perhaps the most simple one of all: Cheer for his niece louder'n you've ever cheered for anything in your life! Compliment her game, but don't put yourself in the position of competing with his niece. It just won't work! You will have more luck if you let her be the star!

The Rabble Rouser

Where to find him: The South, Mississippi to be exact, is well known for its tailgating picnics held yearly at the Grove, a spot on the Ole Miss campus. So if you're just dying to spot a Rabble Rouser in his natural habitat, get a friend to invite you over to campus. But you'll have just as much luck on your home turf if you check out a house party or make a pilgrimage to the local bar, particularly if there is something being celebrated. Another good place to find him is at a concert. Wherever he is, you can expect that he'll be the life of the party. Sounds like a made-in-heaven flirting opportunity!

The approach: If you're tailgating, take along some brownies, or cookies, or something else that will easily fit into the menu. Better yet, bring along some fried chicken, and for goodness' sake, don't forget to bring more beer! Let him be the center of attention. When he tells a story, pay attention and laugh on cue. If he is playing a prank on someone, let him know you're enjoying it. If he is surrounded by people who want to talk to him, step back and let him enjoy his audience.

At a concert, the music will be loud and the crowd huge, so strategically position yourself nearby, gather your wits about you, and put them to work. Share his enthusiasm for the music and try to make some eye contact with him to let him know you "get" why he loves this band.

The Lone Wolf

Where to find him: If there's an open-mike night at your local bookstore or coffee shop, I'm betting you'll find a Lone Wolf. He may be performing one of his masterpieces, or listening to someone else's. He will probably hang out at the local biker bar, or a bar where he knows everyone. This is the type of guy who does not feel comfortable in new environments. He'd rather be at a private event rather than one that is open to the public. For example, if his next-door neighbor is having a barbecue, he'll be there.

The approach: Flirting with a lone wolf is a no-brainer, really. All you have to do is follow his lead and show interest in whatever it is he's doing. Since he usually has a definite idea of what he wants in a girl, you'll do well to be seen and not heard, at least until you know what he's after! A Lone Wolf is picky, picky, picky—that's why he is alone! He will have a "type"—perhaps blond hair, size Ds, and a size 6 or smaller, with no mental health history—if you don't fit his type, just look elsewhere. If you really want this Lone Wolf, when you're hanging out at his favorite bar, quietly send a beer his way, but don't acknowledge that it was you who did. Once he has it figured out and he has approached you, find a way to tell him he's great even if he's not—his mama does that and you need to be in good with Mama! It may seem like a lot of work to get a Lone Wolf, but I hear tell they are worth it if that's what you're after. Ask intelligent questions and listen intently when he launches into a lengthy discussion!

The Mama's Boy

Where to find him: You'll find a Mama's Boy through other people. Maybe he's the son of a friend of your mama's next-door neighbor, or the son of one of your co-workers. He might also have a sister who's looking to find a suitable match for her little brother. The possibilities for finding a Mama's Boy are endless— just start with who you know. You'll never know where it can lead.

The approach: Your flirting skills here will need to include the ability to charm the females as well as the man. If the women attached to the mama's boy like you, there's a pretty good chance he'll like you, too. This means you can skip some of the flirting steps unless you just really *love* flirting! Chat up the girls in his life and remember—be friendly, but don't compete with them for attention—ever!

The Serial Dater

Where to find him: You can find the Serial Dater at a party, chic bar, or the latest, greatest restaurant, as he believes that this is where he'll meet the coolest girls. Check with your local paper or ask your pals to find out where the trendiest spots are, and make a plan to go there.

The approach: I almost hate to tell you more because this guy can't hold on to what he's got. Remember, his motto is that there will always be more silk blouses. So approach with caution! Mention that you've been dying to try this latest spot. Ask him how he heard about it. Blah, blah, blah, you get my drift.

The Prep

Where to find him: No matter where you find the Prep, he'll always be with a large group of friends—who all look, dress, and act just like him. He might be at the country club, drinking scotch at the bar with his college buddies, reliving the good old days, or at a polo match or football game.

The approach: Flirting with a prep can be fun, but flirting with one will be just like flirting with any of them. I'd suggest you pick the prettiest one in the group, and concentrate on him—just don't lose him in the sea of other preps!

The Priss

Where to find him: The Priss will be found anywhere you are liable to enjoy going. He might be found in the designer shoe department of Saks Fifth Avenue. He might be taking a cooking class at the Culinary Institute. You can find him at your favorite spa, trying out the latest face creams and getting a massage.

The approach: He likes what you like, so all you have to do is show interest and enthusiasm. Ask his opinion about the pair of shoes you're trying on. Or ask that he share his recipe for red snapper because his is sooooo much better than yours!

The Southern Heart/Yankee Brain

Where to find him: A Southern Heart/Yankee Brain is pretty easy to find. He loves bookstores and women who are interested in intellectual pursuits. You can find him at the city's ACLU meeting or a political rally.

The approach: The key to the flirting here is to know your subject. A Southern Heart/Yankee Brain is no fool and he can spot a fake a mile away. If you wanna catch this guy, you'd better have a sincere interest in what he's about.

The Southern Gentleman

Where to find him: As for our Southern Gentleman, he can be found just about anywhere, even above the Mason-Dixon line. This Renaissance man has many interests and can join any type of group and fit in. The difference between him and all the others is that he will stand out and won't be consumed by what he's doing. He can be on his way back from a duck hunt, but will have no problem stopping in at a party.

The approach: Because *you* will be his favorite topic, your flirting skills need to be top-notch to get you noticed. Be friendly, approachable, and engaging. Since he will be asking a lot of questions of his own, answer him honestly. Have a sense of humor about yourself, and don't be afraid to tease him just a little. He is looking to see if you are comfortable in your own skin. You're so confident that when he does finally take the bait, you will be the planet around which all the other stars revolve.

Now remember, this little flirting primer will get you well on your way, but like any Southern belle, you have to be ready to think outside the box and improvise when necessary. These steps will work, but use that head of yours to add, change, or leave out whatever you need to do in order to succeed.

Really, really, bad pickup lines to refrain from using

- ❀ "Hey, baby, wanna see my daddy's new truck?"
- ❀ "I believe something just jumped into my undercarriage!" (courtesy of *The Dukes of Hazzard*)
- ❀ "Is that a pencil in your pocket or are you just glad to see me?"
- ❀ "What's your shoe size?" (Y'all know all about this, right?)
- ❀ "Being with you would be like a monkey making love to a skunk—I wouldn't get all I wanted, but I'd get all I could stand!"
- ❀ "After I finish this bucket of beer, wanna give me some sugar?"

Top 5 Southern Belle Flirtin' Props

1. Smile
2. Scent
3. Cleavage
4. *Cleavage!*
5. Push-up bra

CHAPTER FIVE

"I Like My Women Just a Little on the Trashy Side"

The bigger the hair, the closer to God.

—Anonymous

For those of you who are merely beginners in the ways of the South, the title of this chapter is from a song made popular by Confederate Railroad. Basically, the song is implying that many men find their women sexiest when they dress a little flashy and trashy. Southern Belles disagree among themselves about this, but trashy dressing *does* exist, my friends, and it will be addressed in a minute. But first, let's talk about dressing in general.

My mama always said that money does not buy you class or good taste, and she is right about that! Southern women have a distinct way of dressing that gives a hint as to what they're after. But don't let anyone tell you it's easy work being a Southern belle. It's not. But no matter where we hang our hats, we can all stand to learn a few lessons from the Southern belle closet.

Clothing is a large part of our lives, and the way we present ourselves is part and parcel of being a true belle. Clothing has always been much more important in the South because basically, Southern belles have been brought up to be show ponies, for lack of a better way to describe it. We've been instructed by our mamas to dress just trashy enough to get a man all hot and bothered. You see, down here, while a lady's style of dress may give the appearance of being as sweet as that jug of iced tea your granny makes every Sunday, she does so fully knowing that men are enthralled with "nekkidness." And finding a balance between being appropriately dressed and giving him a hint of things to come requires planning.

If you haven't been raised doing it, figuring out the Southern belle dress code will get your knickers in a knot quicker than just about anything! With that said, I have divided Southern dressing codes into two groups: Trashy and tasteful. Keep in mind that there are degrees of trashy—some of which are way worse than others. Also keep in mind that dressing trashy takes just as much effort as dressing tastefully. Or in the words of Dolly Parton, "It takes a lot of money to look this cheap!"

However a Southern belle dresses, she should do the best she can with what she's got, or like the old saying goes, she should hold her head up high even if her pockets are empty!

THE TRASHY CODE

How do you know if you're a trashy dresser?

1. I see London, I see France, I can see your underpants (peeking out of your short, short miniskirt)!
2. Your pushup bra gives you more cleavage than the Grand Canyon!

3. The sound made by your jewelry when you move drowns out your sweet giggle.

4. Your miniskirt can double as a tube top.

5. People think that Aquanet is your signature fragrance!

Now, I have no intention of hurting anyone's feelings here—I'm a Southern belle after all, and I would never speak ill of anybody (at least not to her face). But darlin', the facts are the facts. Trashy dressers are just as talented as the tasteful ones when it comes to attracting men. The only difference is the types of men they attract. So if you're prone to dressing a little on the trashy side, embrace it and the men will come running!

Unlike her conservative cousin, tasteful, there's nothing subdued about a trashy dresser's appearance. Her motto is: "I ain't no fake—take me or leave me! I don't give a @#$*!" Trashy dresses like she does because she wants to be seen, and she's proud of the look she has created. Personally, I think it takes a bunch of confidence to dress trashy. The following is a list of what might be considered part of the trashy dress code.

Tight Clothes

Now, by tight, I mean *real* tight! If you wanna dress this way, you don't need to give a whit about your dress size. If you want to wear a size 8 when you are really a size 12, you know it'll just take a little longer to get dressed. There was this girl in high school named Lottie. Now she was the trashiest dresser I knew at the time. Lottie's daddy used to say her jeans were so tight that if she had a nickel in her back pocket, he could tell whether it was heads or tails!

Tight means showing *lots* of skin. Your skirt should be as short as possible. Just how short, you ask? My friend Lottie says that a man oughta be able to catch a glimpse of a woman's "tu-tu" when she bends over or sits down. You might be shakin' your head about now, but some men really love that. Try getting a denim or leopard-print pattern, but make sure it's short. If you wear a T-shirt, don't be afraid to show the skin between your shirt and pants—a little bit of belly goes a long way. If you don't want to wear a bra, your tank top should allow your breasts to rest comfortably, and if necessary, it's okay if they pour from the armholes. If you aren't getting my point, think of Pamela Anderson. The T-shirt ought to be sparkly or at least have a great saying on the front such as, "I see you looking at me." Remember, the idea is to show skin, lots of skin!

When it comes to pants, if your britches are pretty tight, don't worry if your butt pops out the back of them like the tops of muffins. There are men who find an ample rear to be quite sexy, and if you have one, don't be afraid to show it! If you wish to wear the current trend of low-rise pants, understand that a bit of your pretty little butt is gonna show when you sit or bend over. If you have a tattoo on your lower back, show it off! If when you sit, your stomach is pushing so hard against the zipper of your pants that you look like you'd damn near explode and fly through the air if someone stuck a pin in you to let out the air, you know your pants are just tight enough. Remember, some men like this because, again, the emphasis is on tight, and hints at "a whole lotta woman to love" underneath her clothes!

Underwear

Any great trashy dresser knows that underwear is as much an accessory as a necessity. Men like to get a little peek of what's happening under your clothes—think of it as a way to keep 'em interested! Let's start with your bra. If you're wearing one at all, you must follow the 2-P rule.

What's the 2-P rule, you ask?

1. *Padding*—Whether God gave you AAAs or DDs, a little extra padding never killed anyone.

2. *Push up*—If you don't own a push-up bra, put down this book and march your butt over to Victoria's Secret right now! Ample cleavage is a trashy dresser's greatest asset, so no matter what your cup size, push those puppies up for the world to admire!

As for the panties, if you're going for G-rated, try to find panties with fun slogans on them. For example, if you're going for a cuter look, get your hands on some "day of the week" panties. My friend Lottie's favorite, when she wears panties, say "this could be all yours" across her butt. She swears it makes men swoon— I'm not so sure, but Lottie does seem to have a fair share of men in her life, so maybe I'm misguided. Panty lines are optional for the trashy dresser, but Lottie promises that no man who's attracted to a trashy dresser cares; in fact, some men find those telltale lines to be downright sexy.

But any true trashy dresser knows that when it comes to underwear, it's all about the thong. Trashy dressers often pick the butt-flossing style. Yes, I mean thongs. If you are gonna wear a thong, then please do so with great pride and confidence. If you are a size 6, a size 4 will be better. If you are a size 14, get a 10. You get my drift here? The smaller, the tighter, and the tighter, the better—this is what attracts the male species! According to the trashy dress code, a thong is best worn when it is not hidden, so be sure to wear one that anyone can see—consider it a little decoration for your cute butt!

Lycra and Spandex

Down South, the words *Lycra* and *spandex* are spoken with reverence and awe. Sugar, everybody these days has at least one piece of clothing with a little Lycra or spandex in it. It helps keep the shape and is supposed to enhance the fit. If you don't believe me, check the tag—chances are it'll say "99% cotton, 1% spandex." It's like a minigirdle that smoothes bodily imperfections. And the more you wear, the better it looks. Think sausage. Butchers stuff those things so full that their outer skins are smooth, firm, and bulging. A Southern woman's goal is the same as the butcher's—get it all in there!

Shoes

When it comes to shoes, the higher the better. Get your hands on some four-inch spikes, the kind that cause you to teeter on them precariously even when standing still! Lottie has this habit of looking drunk when she wears high heels because she staggers when she wears them and struggles to keep her somewhat large figure balanced atop a four-and-a-half inch stiletto, but men just love it.

Anyway, aside from sky-high heels, go for adornments that sparkle or that incorporate feathers, buttons, or buckles, animal print, or any other decorative device. If you happen to find a shoe that does all of these things at once, more power to you!

If you're going for a more casual look, flip-flops are one of man's greatest creations, if you ask me. A trashy dresser wears them with anything and everywhere—to church, a party, a funeral, a wedding, wherever. If you're not dressing in high heels, flip-flops are your essential "go-anywhere" accessory.

Hair, Makeup, and Smell-Goods

Whether they're trashy or tasteful, Southern women spend lots of money on their looks.

Hair: Down in the Bible Belt the saying goes, "The higher the hair, the closer to God." With regards to hair, it's time for you to learn the secret every Southern woman already knows: bigger is better. The higher you can tease and back-comb it, the more spellbinding you will be to everyone, so it's time to get reacquainted with your curling iron, and stock your closet with Aquanet.

If you want to adopt the trashy look and plan to dye your hair, don't worry if the roots still show. The man you want to attract will think there's nothing prettier than a woman with Number 46, Ash Blonde hair color with an inch of her real color—black—showing at the roots! If you prefer a more drastic change to your hair color, don't be afraid to bleach it. This should be done not once, not twice, but at least three times to get the "natural" look you want. If in doubt, you can always bleach again!

Makeup: Makeup is a no-brainer for a trashy dresser. More is simply better. Why put on one coat of foundation or dark black eyeliner when three will look positively bewitching? Who cares if purple eye shadow is so yesterday? The color brings out the blue in your eyes, so you *must* wear it. Your "Hussy Red" lipstick needs to scream, "Here I am" and if possible, should be able to be spotted long before the rest of your face comes into view.

Perfume: If you're gonna wear smell-good, there's only one rule to keep in mind: Don't be afraid to use it. If you can't smell your perfume while walking in a strong wind, squirt on a little more. Also, make sure you buy the one cologne that is strong, seductive, and loudly announces your presence. By the way, Lottie's favorite is "Feeling Naughty," in case you want some.

Piercings and Tattoos

Even tasteful dressers have pierced some piece of their anatomy or gotten the occasional tattoo. I'm not saying you shouldn't get one to express yourself through your body. Trashy dressers prefer to take body mutilation to a new level, and the men that love them absolutely adore the body decor! If you go all out, you might have as many as five piercings in one and two in the other ear, along with a tongue ring. You might even want to add a diamond stud to your nose. But you can't stop there. Try piercing your belly button, and get a large piece of jewelry to put through it. After all, why go through the hassle of piercing your navel if no one can see it? There are other places too that you are able to pierce, but I won't mention them here. It makes me blush like a Georgia peach to think of it! All I can say is that your man will appreciate your efforts!

Tattoos are also an intriguing way to express yourself, and men find them to be a great way of figuring out just who you are. For a trashy dresser, one tattoo is considered cowardly. I mean, anyone can have a small heart on their butt, or the peace sign on the inside of an ankle. While you can have those, too, remember that the trashy code insists that bigger, more, and showier is always better. Your man will find you most attractive if you march bravely into that tattoo parlor and have all kinds of things inked on your body in the boldest prints and colors you can find. For example, you might have a bright red blooming rose drawn big as all daylights right across the top of your cheeks (and I don't mean those on your cute little face!). Then, try to get another on your back shoulder that recalls a favorite drinkin' hole that you like to frequent—something like Jack's Saloon—complete with the sign of the bar and Sugar Britches, your nickname there. Your man will find interesting a "bracelet" tattooed on your arm—your upper arm. Not only can this be pretty, but also your man won't feel that he needs to buy you any jewelry! Lottie has a tattoo on her inner thigh of Garfield. Above him is a thought bubble that says "Big fat hairy deal!" What about a reminder of her true love engraved into her arm? This can be a little tricky here considering she might have more than one beau. Lottie's advice here is to get the words "Big Boy" done since it'll cover all your bases with names and such. Besides, it'll make any guy think he's *the* one!

Accessories

A trashy dresser has many accessories to pick from. When it comes to jewelry, anything large, shiny, and noticeable will work. Wear necklaces that have large beads on them, along with a charm that hangs between your marvelous breasts. Wearing many silver or gold chains at the same time will do the trick, too. When it comes to earrings, anything that hangs two to three inches below your earlobe and flaps in the breeze will cause a man's heart to flutter. If they flicker like a large-mouth bass lure, all the better. You could also wear earrings and necklaces that have a holiday theme and light up when you move. Wear several rings on each hand including every "pre-engagement" ring you've had since eighth grade. Toe rings that have a little charm attached to them are an extra special touch. Bracelets should make a lot of noise with the slightest wiggle of your wrist. And don't forget the sexy ankle bracelet to be worn with or without hose, depending on the occasion.

If you carry a purse, the best ones this year are the sparkly kind or the ones with pink, purple, or another color of fur covering them. All the stars are being seen with large metallic bags, so why wouldn't it be appropriate? If you are unsure as to what handbag to carry, the traditional denim tote will be just fine. And if the bottom of your purse smells like the floor of your favorite bar, just douse it with "Feeling Naughty."

Fingernails are another accessory, especially the fake kind. Your nails can be real or artificial but they *must* be very, very long. If you can still use a touch-tone phone with your fingers, those nails are *not* long enough! The polish you wear should reflect your vibrant personality and need not match the color scheme of your wardrobe. Nail embellishments are a perfect way to give your look a unique identity. You might want to consider a little gem that's the color of your birthstone glued to your pinkie nail. You will be the envy of all the other trashy dressers!

The type of man attracted to a trashy dresser is always awed by the props she uses. So get yourself a carton of cigarettes, a box of toothpicks, and bubble gum. Sometimes it can be downright awkward to be standing around in a crowd at a party or on the street, wondering what to do. These items provide you with entertainment while you're waiting to make your next move. You can certainly wow your man with your prowess at making the biggest bubble, popping it, and never hitting your face. He will be so impressed! If you smoke, strategically place a cigarette in the corner of your mouth to give you something to do when you are feeling nervous. If you have a toothpick, use it to preoccupy yourself subtly to prevent you from blurting out something stupid. These props give you something to do and lend a bit of character. (Plus, if you use the toothpick, it can double as a way to get that annoying piece of chicken out of your back tooth!)

The trashy dresser is going to attract a much more adventurous, bold man. It takes a man with great confidence to be seen with a woman who is gonna get all the stares from other men. If you tend to prefer trashier dressing, more power to you. Just be prepared to garner your share of male attention and don't be afraid to show them who you really are!

THE TASTEFUL CODE

You might be thinking that the opposite of trashy will be boring, drab, and unappealing. Not true at all. Where the motto for the trashy code could be "more is more," the motto for the tasteful, Southern dress code could be "less is more." While this is obviously the more subdued of the dressing codes, it is characterized by the belief not only that simplicity is lovely, but also that despite its uncomplicated style, you *will* be able to attract a man. Simply put, the tasteful dresser might appear to be dressing to blend in with a crowd. What you are really doing is letting your personality be the piece of you that stands out. Rather than letting your clothing speak for you, the goal of your dress code is to create a memorable impression rather than overwhelming the senses.

Clothing

The emphasis for the tasteful dresser is on comfort and practicality. A tasteful dresser can dress up or dress down, but the goal is the same—simple elegance. My friend, Weesie, is a quintessential tasteful dresser. She suggests that the first thing you might want to do is to steal a button-down shirt of your brother's or father's. This is one of the most common articles that a tasteful dresser owns. You can wear it with your favorite pair of jeans or without anything else at all! See how a single article of clothing becomes a fashion staple? Just think: a cotton shirt is both useful and sexy. Who'd have thought it?

Every tasteful dresser owns a pair of comfortable, but not necessarily trendy jeans. You are welcome to wear the lowest rise available if that's what you'd like, but keep a classic pair of jeans at hand. Plain, tailored jeans can go just about anywhere. The same goes for khakis. Weesie gets hers at one of those preppy stores, but I hear tell they can be found just about anywhere. She keeps several pairs on hand because they are so versatile.

T-shirts need not be boring, but a tasteful dresser wears one that fits. If she wishes to wear a cropped T-shirt, she will only do so if her abs are pretty smooth. If the T-shirt must have a message on it, it should be from classy places like a ski, golf, or beach resort, or from art museums.

Have you heard the joke that goes like this?

Mama: "Are you fixin' to go to the movies?"
Daughter: "No, why?"
Mama: "Because you're pickin' your seat."

Here's my point. Your shorts need to be long enough that they don't crawl up your butt! This is not attractive to the tasteful dresser. You might like to show off your gorgeous gams, but you have no need to have your cheeks flopping like the tire flaps on an eighteen-wheeler. The same goes with skirts. Short is fine, but the tasteful dresser is not interested in introducing her body to everyone. In other words, *your* tu-tu is *not* for public viewing!

Color is acceptable, but not necessary. You should choose colors that are not overwhelming to the eye. You should be comfortable wearing all black or something with a splash of color. While you wish to be seen by the opposite sex, you do not want to be the proverbial flashing neon sign. All of those flashy, bright, big-flowered items of clothing are fine. If you insist on wearing them, don't wear them all over your body. In other words, if you wear a bright, flowery print on the top, you're better off wearing a solid color on the bottom, or vice versa. Again, the emphasis is on understated adornment.

While I'm talking about clothing, every tasteful dresser in the South has a little black dress that is equally appropriate for wearing to a cocktail party or a funeral. This necessitates that the dress not be too revealing. If it complements your curves, that's fine. Weesie advises that your dress should say "I'm available," not "I'm all hot and bothered, so come and get me." Although you might be all hot and bothered, it's not the tasteful dresser's job to prove it in this dress.

Most tasteful dressers own at least one designer label item, usually a purse. There's nothing wrong with owning a designer brand, but be forewarned: less is more. You need not wear a widely recognized designer coat, carry a purse by another designer, and wear the latest boots by still another. Not only is it tacky, but there is nothing subdued about it. The same goes for wearing a bunch of matching designer pieces that make you look like one big, honking ad for Gucci, for example.

Underwear

Matching underwear is a must for the tasteful dresser. It doesn't have to be the sexiest bra and panties, but it should match. After all, like our mamas taught us: "Dahlin', always wear your best underwear. Why, what in the world would you do if you were in a wreck and had to go to the hospital? What would they think?" I never understood why it mattered if a hospital aide saw me in something less than matching underwear, but I reckon I do understand why you're supposed to wear it when trying to attract a man. First, it makes you feel good so your self-confidence is boosted. Second, if the fella is lucky enough to see your underwear, you don't want to disappoint him.

Thongs are often necessary. First, you'd never go anywhere commando—you just *can't* do it. When wearing a piece of clothing that calls for making sure you have no panty lines, a thong is perfectly appropriate. The color should be flesh-toned so that you don't call negative attention to your bottom.

Shoes

Weesie says that the tasteful dresser will wear fashionable heels, but she is not about to be uncomfortable. She knows that if her feet hurt, she will walk like a duck. Fun is important to her and who can have fun when your dogs are barkin'? Most tasteful dressers have heels and flats, and wear them according to the occasion and outfit. She has a worn-in pair of tennis shoes that are timeless and even though the shoes might be old, they still look good. Sandals are *never* worn with hose, never! A pedicure is preferable, but if you can't keep up with it on a regular basis, a tasteful dresser will keep her unpainted nails clean, short, and tidy. After all, the tasteful dresser wants her man to kiss those little piggies without a second thought. Down here, every tasteful dresser also owns flip-flops. They may have several pairs in bold colors, but they know that wearing them is restricted to certain occasions.

Hair, Makeup, and Smell-Goods

Hair should be neat and regularly styled. While the tasteful dresser won't have an out-of-date hairdo, she doesn't necessarily have to have the latest one, either. The tasteful dresser will pick a style that favors her face because she would rather have a pleasing look than what everyone else has or tells her to do.

Makeup is typically simple. A tasteful dresser understands the importance of makeup, just like the trashy dresser. The tasteful dresser will use just enough to accentuate her features. She loves blush, lipstick, and eye shadow, but she is more reserved when it comes to adding a lot of artificial color. Weesie always says she'd rather wear no makeup rather than spackling it on so thick you have to have a chisel to get it off. Plus, she says that you don't wanna wear so much makeup that you look like a completely different person without it. And how can you make eye contact if your man can only see two caterpillars of mascara?

A tasteful dresser often has a cologne for daytime use and another for nighttime wear. The scents are not heavy, and are usually picked for their ability to create an impression. In other words, a tasteful dresser has a "signature" scent. When a man gets a whiff of it, he will smell that cologne later only to have it remind him of her. But remember what Mama said—if *you* can smell it, you are wearing too much.

Piercings and Tattoos

I only have one piece of advice about piercings here. Truly lovely Southern belles don't do much piercing other than their ears. They've noticed that the number of piercings they have is inversely proportional to where a gal ranks on the 1–10 beauty scale!

Jewelry

The tasteful dresser believes that wearing too much jewelry suggests that you already *have* enough. You should always have an empty left finger. You want to be able to spontaneously try on a ring that catches your eye while you and your man are shopping together! Every Southern-born tasteful dresser that I know owns at least one string of pearls. The pearls don't have to be real, but they sure as heck better look it. They usually have pearl earrings, too. Jewelry for the tasteful dresser is uncluttered. One ring on a finger, two at the most, is enough. There is no need to wear every piece of jewelry you own at one time. The tasteful dresser buys several simple pieces that will go with just about anything. Weesie advises that a pair of diamond studs are the perfect addition to pearls. She says you can travel the world with these two items and always look in fashion.

Which style do you feel describes your way of dressing? Neither dress code is wrong, but merely quite different from one another. Whether you pick "more is more" or "less is more," men will be attracted to you based on your dress code. But it is up to you to help a man get past the "outside" so he is given an opportunity to get to know the real you.

Big, Fat No-Nos

Whether you are a trashy or tasteful dresser, if you are out to get a man, some rules apply to both codes and are nonnegotiable.

❀ Never wear curlers outside of your home.

❀ Never wear bedroom slippers even if it's just down to the corner doughnut shop.

❀ Dress to flatter your own assets no matter what the rest of the crowd is wearing.

❀ Dress according to your age.

❀ Before you leave the house, always look in a mirror.

❀ Don't look at the size tag—either buy for the too-tight or the perfect fit. (You can always cut the size out if you must!)

❀ If you don't want to be characterized as a slut, don't dress like one unless you want to be, and then more power to you!

❀ Stand up straight.

❀ Never "pick" at anything in public—your pants, your crotch, your teeth, your ears, your nails, your pimples.

❀ Just because it comes in your size does not mean you have to buy it.

Top 5 Things Every Southern Belle Should Have in her Closet

1 LBD (Little Black Dress)

2 Sexy, high heel sandals (and pedicure to match!)

3 An old barn jacket or hunting jacket (says "I'm able to be casual and game for a walk in the woods")

4 Tight jeans

5 The "impress the mother" church-style outfit

CHAPTER SIX

Smooth as Butter

Scarlett O'Hara didn't think she was manipulating. That's just the way she got what she wanted.

—Donna Mills

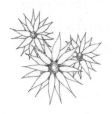

Making others feel special is as natural to a Southern belle as drinking a gin and tonic on a hot summer day. You see, our mamas taught us that the way we treat others says more about us than anything else. It defines the very substance of a Southern belle and what is important in her life.

I can hear some of you saying, "But what about taking care of *yourself*?" Ladies, no one said we don't pay attention to ourselves—have you seen the size of our cosmetic bags? Having the ability to make others feel comfortable and cared for is at the heart of being a traditional Southern belle. Some call it charm, some call it grace, still others call it home training. Whatever label you choose, it all boils down to one thing: etiquette.

We are lookin' to get us a man, right? Part of snagging a good one is to learn the etiquette of making him feel extraordinary. Learning this skill might take practice, but anyone with determination and a little motivation can do it. Once you get down the etiquette of dating, you'll have him eating out of the palm of your hand and begging like a puppy for your affection!

Every true Southern belle owns an etiquette book (just in case there's something she wasn't *born* knowing, such as the difference between a tablespoon and dessertspoon!). But there's another side to knowing proper etiquette. Being smooth as butter allows us to get away with just about anything! I have seen many a belle say "f### you" to a man with nothing more than a smile or the wink of an eye. The beauty of it, though, lies in the fact that when she does this, she leaves him wondering, "What exactly was she trying to say to me?" For example, let's say a man is trying to buy you a drink. Now, you don't find him the least bit attractive but you really want that drink. Glance in his direction with a small smile, accept the drink, and then turn your head in the other direction. This should communicate to him that you are not interested in his advances. A man may not necessarily get the message the first time, but any man raised in the South ought to catch on sooner or later. Some may call that playing games, but not me. I call it having a code of behavior—in dating and in all aspects of life—that necessitates using your wits and charm to get what you want without unnecessarily hurting or humiliating your man.

THE SOUTHERN BELLE'S PRIMER FOR THE ETIQUETTE OF DATING

1. **Everyone deserves to be treated with respect and kindness, at least in the beginning.** Let's face it; as much as we think we know how to read people, we're not always correct in our judgments. When meeting men, you should give each and every one of

them a chance before you discard them like yesterday's trash. The more you treat them graciously and genially, the quicker you are apt to see what lies in their true character. Southern belles are so good at making others feel important that it not only serves to disarm people, it also makes them want to tell you everything about themselves. Once that happens, you've got all the information you need to separate the bulls from the bullshitters. So until a man bores you to death and makes poking your eye out with a stick sound more enticing than watching him draw another breath, please do your best to be accommodating and pleasant.

So what to do when a man doesn't deserve your good intentions? Well, I guess there are all sorts of things you *could* do. You could be all over him like white on rice and have one big duck fit to let him know how you feel, but what for? Some men are just dumb as hell, bless their hearts, and you needn't waste your time. But there's no need to be rude. Who knows? He may be a complete idiot but he might have a delicious cousin for you to meet. I say you walk away and hold on to your dignity.

Remember my friend, Mary, who married the pig farmer, TJ (Thomas Junior), from Arkansas? Well, my other friend Edna Louise swore and be damned that she would not go to their wedding, not because she was against the wedding, but because she was still getting over the "trauma" of a horrible blind date that TJ had sent her on. The date was with TJ's best bud, RD (I don't think the initials really stood for anything—he was just RD). Anyway, Edna Lou did not think that a Sonic burger and a night of pool and darts were quite up to her first date standards. (So maybe RD actually stood for Real Dumb!) But did Edna Louise tell RD how she felt? Heck, no! She was delightful, but not overly so. She said she found the Sonic to be an "interesting choice," and sure enough, she ordered a small burger. She played pool and darts with enough enthusiasm not to be rude. When the date was over, she remarked to RD that this had been the "most unique date" she'd ever been on and she appreciated his kindness. She was so "sweet" to RD that he could not stop singing her praises even though she had made it clear that no future dates or prospects in RD's future would include her. Nevertheless, we dragged her, kicking and screaming, to the "pig roast" and wedding. Well, guess who showed up? RD and his twin brother, JP (not identical by any means), a successful commercial real estate broker from Atlanta who took quite a shine to Edna Louise right away. Well, the rest is history, and needless to say, it wasn't long before we all had to travel to the Little Rock Country Club for the very proper wedding reception of Mister JP and Mrs. Louise (she dropped the Edna quickly). The moral of the story: A Southern belle never burns her bridges.

2. **You catch more flies with honey than with vinegar.** Certain "progressive" women—and you know who you are!—will tell you that you should demand what you want from a man and not back down until you get it. My friend Judy, the New Yorker, is just like that. We went to this fancy restaurant known for being a celebrity hot spot. We didn't have reservations, but Judy walked up to the maître d', demanded a table, and palmed him a twenty.

The wait, he said, would be an hour. I could feel the tension mounting and, like a true Southern belle, I immediately began to smooth things over.

"It's all right, sir," I flashed my most sugary smile, gently touched him on the wrist, and gave a roll of the eyes to signify my friend was out of bounds.

Now, it was clear to me that the maître d' couldn't've given a rat's ass about us. Judy was treating him like a servant, and even the person lowest on the company totem pole appreciates some respect. I decided to try the old Southern charm. I leaned in close and gave him my brightest smile. "Sorry she's being such trouble. It must be the divorce. Mercy me, she caught her husband in bed with her best friend and now he's suing her for divorce! I came all the way up here from Memphis and told her I wanted to take her somewhere she's never been, and she picked your pretty restaurant here." Okay, so I lied like a damn dog, but it worked! Within minutes, the maître d' was leading us to a prime table right by the window, asking me about Graceland (tell 'em you're from Memphis and that's the first thing anyone wants to know about!), and pointing out Denzel Washington eating a salad. So there! The moral of this story is that you don't have to be a bitch to get what you want, and sometimes it's downright counterproductive!

3. Never let him see you sweat. I don't mean this literally, although no one really wants to see you perspire, or as our mamas say, "glisten." It's about holding your head up high with aplomb and the conviction that you are the prettiest thing in the room.

Make a bold entrance. In a restaurant, smile at those admiring you and nod pleasantly. At a party, say hello to everyone you know. If across the room you spot your old heartthrob with his new fiancée, for heavens' sake *don't* slam your hand to your throat, mutter a quivering "Oh my god!" and head for the ladies' room. Not only is this rude to your date, but it makes you look like a simpering adolescent. Instead, take a deep breath, inconspicuously wipe the beads of sweat from your face, and find yourself a fan or a cold drink.

Another instance that might make you "glisten" more than just a little bit is if you unexpectedly run into the boy-now-man who deflowered you at age seventeen. One does *not* point this out to one's date, for God's sake. Or what if you are introduced to your date's ex-girlfriend—a gorgeous, perky-assed, leggy creature? Should you hide in the corner and pout? No, ma'am! This is a perfect situation in which to turn on your newly acquired Southern belle charm: "Oh, yes! John has *mentioned* you to me. I'm so *glad* to finally have an ass; I mean face, to go with your name! You are just *precious*!" Grown women hate being called precious, like they are some kind of Pekingese mix. But it's a great Southern belle way to call someone a bitch!

If greeting and meeting others makes you "glisten" with nervousness, try some of these techniques. Make sure you make frequent eye contact with your date so he doesn't feel neglected. If you're flirting with another man (because let's face it, it's always good to hedge your bets!), toss your date a wink to let him know he's still the focus of your evening. A wink is worth a thousand words and can convey anything from "I've got it under control" to "I'll be with *you* later" or, as mentioned earlier, "F#&* you." Any way you use it, a wink suggests *confidence* and no one will ever notice your "glistening."

When you leave, make a graceful exit even if you are not feeling very self-assured. Even if you are just going to powder your nose, politely excuse yourself. If you are departing for good, thank your date for a lovely evening and make your good-byes. The trick is to never make your date feel excluded from your attention. Your goal should be to enchant him and leave him spellbound by your presence, no matter how uncomfortable, nervous, or uncertain you may be!

4. Provide him with the illusion that <u>he's</u> in charge. Men love to think they are in control of all situations, but we Southern women are well aware that this is just plain silly. Remember, Southern belles are charming, not stupid. Letting a man think he is master of his domain is critical to his self-esteem. Why should we shatter their happy illusions?

Let's say your date suggests that you go to a particular restaurant, adding that he knows you'll love it. And let's say you've been to that place before, and you'd rather eat a bar of soap than go there. What do you do? You've got two choices as I see it:

Choice #1: You can take the downright blunt approach and respond with, "There's no way in hell I'd want to go there." However, this violates rules #1, 2, and 4 of the Southern Belle Etiquette Primer, and a real Southern belle would never consider this option.

Choice #2: You tell him it sounds great and go anyway because maybe it won't be so bad this time. And if that's just too passive for you, you can try yet another option.

Choice #3: You agree, wait a minute or two, and then mention another restaurant you'd really like to go to. If he has some sense, he'll catch on and ask if you'd rather go there, thus providing you with the opportunity to say, "Why, that might be fun. If you think it's a good idea, let's do it." All of a sudden, it has become *his* idea. Easy as pie. The moral here? Use your brain and find a way to keep from completely humiliating him—this will get you further than you'd ever expect.

5. When in doubt, imitation is the best form of flattery. When trying to impress your date, don't be afraid to ask questions and follow his lead. If he invites you to dinner, for example, ask how you should dress. You don't want to put on your prettiest party dress only to find out you're going to a barbecue joint. Likewise, you wouldn't want to be caught in your cute, distressed blue jeans and new retro "Lucky Charms" T-shirt if you are dining at a chic restaurant. Before you order, find out what he finds interesting on the menu and what he might order. This is a good way to find out how much money he is planning on spending. If he picks something less expensive, don't you go and order the priciest thing on the menu. That just shows poor breeding, my mama would say. Perhaps he doesn't have a lot of money, but wants to impress you. Or he might have plenty of cash, but really *does* want what he is getting. There's just no way to know for sure and a Southern belle wouldn't be caught dead asking.

Here's a safe strategy—one of two choices. First, you can order modestly from the menu with the simple explanation that you really do love chicken. You can always hit the ice cream and peanut butter at home after the date. Or (and I swear this works), you can just say, "I would love it if you would order something for me and help me eat it." Now this does a couple of things—it lets him know you're not afraid of letting him "be in charge," and it let's you know how considerate he may be—after all, if he really does love liver and onions and doesn't care whether you do or not, this may be a warning sign.

Likewise, if he orders a drink, certainly you can, too. But what if he doesn't drink? Again, it's hard to tell if it's because he's some sort of athlete who believes his body is a temple or because he's a recovering alcoholic. For God's sake, don't ask. What if he gets drunk? Okay, if you really want to, go ahead and join him. But find a designated driver or stay sober. It doesn't bode well for a potential "keeper" to get a DUI on the way home. After all, what Southern belle wants to step foot inside a jail just to see this guy again? (And if he gets plastered because he's confident *you* will drive, well this boy needs a parent, not a date—and certainly not a second date!)

But here is the real answer—always stay a couple of paces behind him—*no, I'm not talking about walking down the damn sidewalk*—pay attention here. I don't care if you have just gotten rescued off the lifeboat from the *Titanic* and have not eaten for a week, do not—*I said, DO NOT*—clean your plate! Always leave some of everything, from the soup to the dessert. I don't care what your mama told you about the starving orphans in China—they are not going to fly in just to finish your supper, and they will not help you in your quest for the perfect man.

The bottom line here is this: Men love to think that whatever it is they've done is the most perfect, greatest thing on earth. Imitating or following his lead is a simple technique to communicate to him that you think he's marvelous!

6. You have two eyes and two ears—use them twice as much as your mouth. One of the best ways to let a man know you are interested in him is to look and listen. When he talks, watch his face, look him in the eye, and really listen. Men love to talk about themselves, so all you really have to do is be inquisitive and he'll be off and running.

There's much you can learn about him through your observations. Does his face light up when he talks about his family? Does he get more excited telling you about the buck he killed and skinned than about the last book he read? Does he think he's God's gift to the universe or is he more humble? Does he ask about you or is it all about him? These are clues, girls, as to what he thinks about himself and what he cherishes most.

About now, you might be asking, "But what if he is boring?" Yep, we've all had those dates where we are afraid the evening will never end. The goal of dating is to get a chance to meet all sorts of men, which means the chances of you getting a dullard in the mix are pretty high. A Southern belle masters the art of *appearing* to be intrigued by what a man is saying, while all the time her brain is somewhere else.

You can survive a tedious date by looking right at him and imagining him as bald, bearded, with a nose ring, with Paul Newman's eyes—whatever you have to do to entertain yourself. But whatever you do, don't have a look on your face that suggests you'd rather tear off your nails than sit there with him. That would be rude and unnecessary—after all, it's one date, and no one is forcing you to go out with this imbecile again. (But don't forget, be sweet—he might just have a killer cousin!)

7. Pump him up. Men love to talk about themselves. Ask about his interests, talents, and work. Try not to ask questions that can be answered yes or no, because that will make for a lot of work for you. As he talks, the more you make him feel he's the king of the world—at least for tonight—the more entertaining your date will be. Comments such as "You are so smart" or "How accomplished you are!" are always useful. Just say anything that plays to his interests and perceived talents! You may think this is sucking up, but I disagree. It's just a hallmark of Southern graciousness. The rest of the country could stand to suck up so beautifully! A Southern belle shows her true character by being tolerant of others' differences. By doing this, you might find out you have a lot in common and that behind his reticent exterior is a quite passionate fella. Of course, you also run the risk of discovering he's just plain as white bread. Either way, by pumping him up and drawing him out, you can uncover important information that will allow you to decide whether to reel him in further or throw him back to the sea.

You can pump him up by making him feel needed. Let him open your car door. Yes, I know you are perfectly capable of doing it. Perhaps you can ask him how a word on the menu is pronounced, or what he thinks about some recent trend. You're probably reading this with your mouth hanging open as if you're catchin' flies, thinking, "How can she say that? We are not helpless creatures." You are right; we are most definitely not helpless. But that is not the point. Men are way more helpless than we ever fear to be (or they think we are), but they don't know it and there's absolutely no benefit to be had from telling them this. It has been driven into their little brains that they are the dominant sex and are better than women at just about everything. The only way we conquer this is to let them have small victories, like opening a car door, or screwing in a lightbulb. Not only is it entertaining to watch a man fall all over himself to do something for you that he thinks you can't do, but it is also loads of fun to let him think he is totally great at it. And it's really no skin off our noses, is it?

8. Don't share too much history. While it's perfectly acceptable for you to answer his questions and ask some of your own, don't go too far. Your date does not need to know the details of your last breakup or that your Uncle Ed cheated on your aunt with a second cousin and now the whole family's in an uproar. He doesn't have to be privy to your family's sordid details when it comes to marriages, divorces, twelve-step groups, and the like. I mean, imagine if he were to disclose that his mama, bless her heart, just got out of the loony bin and that they think she'll be okay *this time*. Wouldn't you be caught off guard just a little?

Keep a bit of mystery going about yourself as long as you can. Part of the fun of dating is taking the time to get to know someone. Once you've decided he's worth it, *then* you can begin to divulge some of the bad stuff.

9. Keep your cell phone use to a minimum. I would hope you don't need much advice in this area. Talking on your phone during a date is rude, inconsiderate, and downright aggravating! Girls, my advice would be to take your phone with you in case of an emergency. But don't plant the sucker on the table with the ringer on—even if you *are* hoping for a phone call to rescue you from the poor gentleman you are with. Keep it in your purse with the ringer either off or on vibrate and check it on a mid-date trip to the ladies' room. If you absolutely *must* be available to someone for a reason, please explain that to your date ahead of time. If you absolutely must take a call, keep it short and get back to your date. No man likes to be treated as if he were invisible, so get yourself under control when it comes to the phone!

10. Remember your table manners. This might sound obvious, but you'd be surprised at how some people forget their home training so quickly. Chew with your mouth *fully* closed even if he doesn't.

Do *not* talk with your mouth full. It is simply gross, and food has a tendency to fly out when you least expect it. My friend Maisie was on a first date with a guy that she really liked. As they were eating their salads, they were talking about her puppy dog, Rufus, and she got so excited that a piece of a carrot shot out of her mouth and landed on her date's chin. Maisie was horrified, but there was no way she could undo what she'd done. Needless to say, the guy didn't call her again, and the only date Maisie had for the next couple of weeks was with sweet little Rufus.

In terms of minding one's manners, Southern belles shouldn't have to be reminded about this, but we all have lapses in our judgment at times. Never, and I cannot stress this enough, *never* pick or suck your teeth at the table. Now I know most of you are saying "I would never do that!" Yeah, yeah, we've all done it, sister, but we don't have to be proud of it. The sucking noise you might make while trying to vacuum the food from your teeth is not subtle. And don't think you can hide what you're doing by using your little finger. You may be convinced that you can delicately pull something from your back teeth that way and that no one will notice, but believe me, you are not nearly as crafty as you believe. Your silverware is likewise not a tool for your dental hygiene, nor is a mouthful of water to be power-swished at the table. And do I need to even mention toothpicks? I hope not, but I wanna cover all the bases. Get up from the table, excusing yourself of course, and go to the damn ladies' room! There you can suck, pick, and do whatever else you like in privacy.

A word about gum and cigarettes: If you *must* smoke, first ask your date (if he's not smoking), if it would bother him if you have a cigarette. Find a way to avoid blowing smoke in his direction even if he's smoking, too. Besides, every Southern belle knows that it's bad manners, if not a bit mannish, to hook her elbow over the back of her chair! Maybe this is a personal thing with me, but if you want to smoke, keep it to yourself. And for God's sake, don't sit there with a cigarette stub hanging in your mouth. Need I say more?

Gum? Just say no. I don't know about you, but I have a hard time *not* smacking gum when I have it. Gum is fun and I like to blow bubbles. Neither smacking nor blowing bubbles is polite—in the South, it is considered thoroughly tacky!

While it does not personally offend me if someone applies lipstick at the table, it is poor form and bad manners. Your date doesn't really need to see you put on your war paint. My friend Mary Jane has a technique where she pretends to be retrieving something from the floor and quickly, surreptitiously, freshening her lipstick. But she is quick and very accurate with her aim, so unless you've had years of practice, have some class and take it to the bathroom!

11. Be responsive even when you don't want to be. When a man is nervous, he may tell the same story or joke a couple of times. This is not the time to act like your mama and say something like, "Honey, you just told me that," or, "Hell's bells, Burt, no one wants to hear that again!" Give the poor boy a break, at least on the first date. If he really is anxious, it might be a compliment to you. He wants to make a good impression, but just can't keep track of what he's saying on 'count of your being so mesmerizing. So smile, laugh, do whatever is appropriate to make him comfortable. Now, on the other hand, if this behavior continues through several dates, you might have a problem on your hands. He might not have a lot of "material" to discuss, or maybe he's a consummate bore. In either case, remember the Southern belle way—there's no need to make him feel dumber than a bucket of rocks.

12. It's okay to complain, but don't be a bitch. A man has a way of taking it personally when you complain about something like poor service in a restaurant. But If you feel you must complain, do it politely and skip the rudeness.

If you're at a fancy-pants place that your date thought you'd like, and you don't like what you ordered, you have two choices. You can smile, say nothing, and choke your food down with extra wine. Or you can politely call the waiter to your table and say something like, "I believe I ordered the fish rather than chicken. Would it be too much trouble to exchange this?" Complaining is best done by leaving the bitchiness out. Why? Because all your poor date wants is to treat you to a lovely evening. Complaining loudly and attacking the waiter will leave your date feeling like it is his fault that dinner was not perfect. The humiliation he may feel is likely to linger and he may not be able to bring himself to call you and try again. Dating is hard.

13. Let him outdrink you, at least the first few times. I'm gonna let you in on a secret. Down here, we love to have a drink or two, and many a Southern belle has been known to drink a man under the table. Now we do it with style and in a ladylike fashion, mind you, but we can be quite competitive when we want. On a date, however, remember that you are trying to make a good impression. This is not the time to show him how many gin and tonics you can down chased by shots of tequila. Believe me, you "dumb up" a bunch when you're drinking, and the things that come out of your mouth might not be the sort of information you intended to impart. You're also not nearly as funny as you think. Then there's also the chance that you might, ahem, get sick, or pass out. What a wonderfully tacky way to begin a potential relationship! Just trust me on this—keep your wits about you and save the heavy drinking for another time.

14. If he's rude on the first date, he'll be rude for the rest of your life. There are a couple of things that you should always consider when picking a man. First, if your man is unnecessarily rude to anyone while you are out with him, take this as a sign. If he will act like that on your first date or two, chances are it will only get worse. Second, if he doesn't respect you, run. There are many men out there just waiting to be swept up by your new-found Southern charm and irresistibility!

OUT WITH THE OLD WAYS!

Now that you've learned the dos of dating, there are a few antiquated dating rules that should be put out to pasture:

1. **Toss the "Keep 'em waiting" rule.** According to this old rule, you were supposed to "keep 'em waiting awhile" so they would appreciate their chance to have a date with you.

For example, Liz met Jeff at the door in a rather sexy dressing gown, pointed him to the bar, and said a very sugary voice, "Just give me a minute and I'll be ready to go." Now all Liz really had to do was put on her dress, panty hose, and shoes and she'd be ready (in fact she *was* fully ready, but undressed so she could go through the waiting game with Jeff). So eighteen minutes later (after a phone call with a girlfriend, a *Cosmo* article, and two purse changes), Liz emerged from the bedroom only to find Jeff's empty drink glass, but no Jeff. Of course, Liz was enraged with Jeff though she should've directed her anger at dear old mama. When she finally got Jeff on the phone, all he would say was, "Liz, I'm sorry, this just won't work." That was it.

2. **Don't keep them waiting with the "12-minute" rule.** I ran into Jeff a couple of months later and happened to ask him about

Liz. Jeff told me he couldn't date a woman who violated the 12-minute rule. He said "Who was the crazy woman that invented the 'keep 'em waiting' rule?" Then he told a story about when he was dating this girl, Ellen. Evidently, she was always late and kept him waiting. They always missed the first few minutes of the movie, or were late for dinner reservations. One morning after he stayed over at her place, they were awakened by Ellen's friend Jill's call at eight thirty, announcing a big sale at their favorite shoe store. By eight forty-two, Ellen was dressed and out the door to meet Jill. Twelve minutes! He decided that if a date with him and being on time is not more important than a shoe sale, then he should be out the door. He has a point.

3. Ditch the "Don't make the first move" rule. You've got to handle this very gently, but it *is* okay to call him up and ask him to do something. Think about it—this is the reason all of those sweet southern sororities have all of those fancy formals. It is the one time the unattached girls can reach out and ask a guy out without any risk of its being a social no-no. So if you're interested, don't be afraid to make a gentle first move. More times than not you'll find that the guys are really shy and can be very receptive.

4. Do not adhere to the "I should accept his last-minute invitation because he'll never call again" rule. If he wants a date with you for Friday or Saturday, he'd better call before Tuesday. If he calls at 11:30 P.M. and wants to "drop by," do not let him (unless, of course, he's one of those "friends with benefits"). Calling earlier indicates that he has been thinking of you and can't wait to see you.

5. Don't be desperate. There's nothing worse than the smell of fear or desperation on a woman. It may have been a while since you've had a date, or at least a date worth telling your friends about. But for heaven's sake, resist the urge to blurt out to your date that "I don't care what we do, I'm just so glad to finally be out of the house." A man is attracted to the woman he thinks is in demand. He wants a challenge, not a slam dunk!

Top 5 Things a Southern Belle Never Does on a Date

1 Apply make-up at the table

2 Chew with her mouth open

3 Talk about old boyfriends

4 Take a nonemergency cell phone call

5 Mention marriage

CHAPTER SEVEN

The Deviled Egg Plate

Southerners can't stand to eat alone. If we're going to cook a mess of greens we want to eat them with a mess of people.

—Julia Reed

HAH! I betcha you Yankee gals are scratching your heads wondering what in the hell a deviled egg plate is. There really *is* such a thing as a deviled egg and a deviled egg platter, but we'll get to that later.

For now, you should know that the deviled egg plate is a metaphor for Southern hospitality. It goes with everything—just like a pretty ol' smile.

You see, in the South, hospitality is what we do best and when it comes to courting a man, there are four things you'll need to keep in mind: attention, generosity, gratitude, and food. You see, hospitality feeds the heart *and* the stomach. Even though men can be thick as bricks, they recognize hospitality when they see it, and it makes them feel special. It's so easy to do, and it can melt any man's heart.

Attention

You remember what I said in the last chapter about having two eyes and two ears, but only one mouth? A Southern belle makes her man feel special by focusing her attention on him and making him feel special. For example, my sorority sister, Tracylyn, had a best friend named Mable. This gal Mable arranged a double date for herself and her boyfriend, Sam, and with Tracylyn and a new lawyer in Sam's office named Adam. When Tracylyn met Adam for the first time, she knew this was a man she'd like to date more than once. From the minute she met him, she began the subtle art of observing his every move. She saw that he was left-handed and asked to sit where she wouldn't be in the way of the others. She silently registered the kind of beer he liked along with the way he asked for his steak to be cooked, and how he had a real liking for Tabasco sauce. She noticed that when Sam made a joke about a rather large secretary in the office, Adam came to her rescue. She listened as Adam talked about Jake, the puppy he'd just adopted from the pound. She watched as he talked to the waiter and how gracious he was when served. She noticed that when she talked, he looked at her as if she were the only person in the room speaking. Well, you get my drift.

When Adam asked her out for a second date, she put the information she'd learned to good use. As they approached a booth, she asked which side would be most comfortable for him. He was surprised that she remembered he was left-handed. As the evening unfolded and their food arrived, she asked for Tabasco and then passed it to him, saying she knew he loved the stuff. She inquired about Jake and how Adam was adapting to having a new puppy.

While all of this might sound trite, think about a time where someone treated you with that sort of attention. Although women like to feel noticed and special, men find it intoxicating. Try it—I swear it works. And although a woman is thought to be much better at this skill than a man, just know you've got a real winner if your guy pays attention to all the little things that make you tick!

Generosity

Southern belles are some of the most big hearted people on this green earth. They are unsparing in their time, attention, and their deeds for others. It just comes naturally. If a neighbor is going to a big party and hasn't the time to get the proper dress, count on a Southern belle to offer one of hers. If a friend has been dumped, a Southern belle is first on the scene to comfort her with ice cream, alcohol, and tissues. If your mama just got out of the hospital, a Southern belle will interrupt her schedule to make her famous chicken salad and deliver it to her complete with crackers, paper plates, and iced tea.

Generosity is also about kindness. Southern belles treat everyone with respect and graciousness even if they don't deserve it. If you want to capture a man's heart, develop a generous heart and actions. If he is sick, make him soup and take it to him. If he is upset about something, empathize with him and ask how you might cheer him up. In Tracylyn's case, when Adam invited her to dinner at his house for the first time, she took a dessert for Adam and a bone for his dog Jake. Halfway through dinner Jake tried to consummate his own relationship with Tracylyn by humping her leg. Needless to say, Adam was embarrassed and immediately apologized. Tracylyn was horrified, but you'd never know it. She smiled, told Adam not to worry, and said that Jake was just being a dog. Adam couldn't get over it and reported next day to Sam that she was the kindest, nicest girl he'd ever met and hoped he could hold on to her despite Jake's poor behavior! You see, the generosity shown by Tracylyn had nothing to do with the giving of a gift. It was about making sure Adam didn't feel embarrassed or uncomfortable.

Gratitude

Southern belles are always saying "thank you" in one way or another. While it may sound ingratiating, we *really do* mean it. How do we do it? My mama writes thank-you notes for everything, big or small. My friend Anne takes cookies or homemade toffee. Another girl I know takes a small gift when invited for dinner or a weekend at a beach house. No matter what form the gesture takes, you can be sure it is accompanied by a sugary, heartfelt "Thaaaaaank ya."

Those two little words carry a lot of weight and tend to make people feel valued and cherished. So when it comes to dating, the same rule applies. Be appreciative, grateful, and savor whatever the moment presents. Never forget that your man has a fragile ego, so finding a way to say you treasured your time with him will earn you big points!

Food

Down here it's a known fact that one of the quickest ways to a man's heart is through his stomach. A man's mama started this when he was a mere baby. If a son showed delight in a particular dish his mama made, she would get out her recipe box and put it under a file that said "my baby's favorites." Whenever she wanted to dote on him, cheer him up, or celebrate, she'd make those dishes. Often she had a special platter or serving dish that she used only for these particular recipes.

Well, naturally, with a mama like that, it's no wonder a man equates food with love and affection. It's pretty easy to please a man with food, so I suggest you learn how to cook *something*. And if you truly have no desire to get anywhere near a kitchen, you better know how to take that Kentucky Fried Chicken out of its box and serve it up on your best china! In my younger days, I was known to put Stouffer's Lasagna in a baking dish and present it to a boy I liked as if it were my own. We've all done it, and it's okay, but I think we can do better than that. In every Southern belle's recipe box, she has some staple menu items: chicken salad; deviled eggs; fried chicken; biscuits; corn bread; homemade mayonnaise; chess pie and banana puddin'; and of course, sweet iced tea. Learn to make just one of these and you'll be way ahead of the game!

Here's another way that food is going to play into your dating life—like it or not, sooner or later, he is going to want to cook dinner for you. Now some men can cook anything and do it well, but men can hardly manage with a can opener, let alone get the grill going. Here's what you need to know—no matter how bad it may be, he is going to think it is great! He'll be burstin' with pride and think he's a culinary genius if he thinks to add Worcestershire sauce to a can of Beanie Weenies. You're on your own here—I know we girls fake a lot of things for our men, so if your appetite is one of them, you go girl. But I sure hope that your chosen one can cook like Emeril rather than Chef Boyardee.

Chicken salad is yummy and there are various ways to make it. Men like it, I think, because it seems to be an acceptable form of "salad," more manly, I guess. Some make it with chicken, mayo, onions, and celery. Others add grapes and nuts to theirs. However she makes it, every Southern woman I know thinks hers is the best. Some even refuse to share their recipes as if it's a security breach to reveal it. I remember a story my stepson told me. He was dating this girl named Tiffany (I know, what can I say?) and she was really wanting to impress him. He'd told her about his mama's chicken salad, so she called up his mama to ask for the recipe. Would you believe his mama refused to give it to her? We've laughed about this over the years, but evidently, there's some secret ingredient in hers and she's not giving it up for anyone, not even for her son! Personally, I think she refused to give it up because of her name. Tiffany is a Yankee and no Southern mama is going to ruin a perfectly good chicken salad recipe by putting it in the hands of a Yankee!

I'm gonna share some of my time-tested recipes that are sure to tickle your man's fancy. If you try any of these, I swear on my knickers that you'll have him eating out of the palm of your hand in no time!

Homemade Mayonnaise

I bet you wonder why in the hell anyone would make their own mayonnaise. I'll also bet those of you who ask that have never had it. Homemade mayonnaise is some of the best stuff God ever invented. It goes on just about anything: your ham sandwich, in your chicken salad, on your tomatoes. It's a little tricky to make, but if you are feeling brave, most men are pretty impressed that you took the time to make something you could have easily bought but that tastes twenty times better!

> **Juice of 1 lemon**
> **1 egg, at room temperature**
> **1 scant teaspoon salt**
> **1 scant teaspoon paprika**
> **2 level teaspoons prepared mustard**
> **2 cups vegetable or canola oil**
> **1½–2 tablespoons cider vinegar**

1. Mix together the first five ingredients in a mixing bowl.

2. Beat with an electric mixer at high speed to blend, then slowly add the salad oil in eight to ten additions.

3. When this is done, cut the speed to low and add the cider vinegar.

Now if you just can't bring yourself to make the real thing, try adding sour cream to taste to your favorite commercial brand of mayonnaise. It really helps the texture and will at least taste homemade!

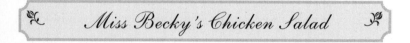

Miss Becky's Chicken Salad

I'm not as proprietary about my chicken salad and I'm happy to share the recipe with you. When I fixed it for my boyfriend, he loved it, and now he's my husband! Feel free to add your own special touch to it, but it's pretty damn good all on its own. The sweet pickle juice is the secret to this wonderful comfort food! Serve it with bread, crackers, or just all by itself.

> **4 chicken breasts**
> **3 hard-boiled eggs, chopped**
> **1 cup chopped celery**
> **½ cup chopped onion**
> **½ cup mayonnaise (homemade is best!)**
> **¼–½ cup chopped sweet pickles**
> **⅓ cup sweet pickle juice**
> **1 teaspoon salt**
> **½ teaspoon pepper**

1. Boil the chicken breasts until the meat is fallin' off the bones. Let it cool a bit. Pull the chicken off the bones as if you were shredding it, and place in a large mixing bowl.

2. Add the chopped eggs, celery, onion, salt, and pepper to the chicken, and give the salad a good stir.

3. Add the mayonnaise, pickles, and pickle juice a little at a time, to taste. If you can, refrigerate it overnight before serving.

To-Die-For Deviled Eggs

Okay, okay, I know you are just dying with desire to know about this deviled egg thing. I'm not sure I even get the mystique about it. What I *can* tell you is that men have always eaten them up as fast as you can serve them. My son-in-law is from California of all places, and he can eat half a dozen without stopping to take a breath, so there must be something to it! Oh yeah, if you're serving deviled eggs, don't forget the ever-popular egg platter. This is a special dish with egg-shaped indentations designed to cradle half of an egg. Almost every Southern girl I know has one—mine has a funky chicken standing in the middle. My mama's is much more formal and elegant. Whatever your preference, get one. It's real hard to serve these little suckers on a regular plate since they have a tendency to slide all over the place!

6 eggs

1 teaspoon prepared yellow mustard (homemade is
   best!)

5 teaspoons mayonnaise

Sweet pickle juice

Sweet pickles and/or pimientos, for garnish

1. Hard-boil the eggs, let them cool, peel them, and cut them
in half.

2. Scoop out the yolk from each egg into a food processor
bowl. Add the mustard and about half of the mayonnaise. Process
the mixture until smooth.

3. I add the pickle juice before the remaining mayo because I
like its sweet taste. Add it a little bit at a time until the egg mixture is just the way you like it. If needed, add the remaining mayonnaise as necessary to keep it thick. This is a trial-and-error kind
of thing, so if you get it too thin, just boil another egg or two and
add that yolk to your recipe.

4. Using a spoon, heap the mixture into each egg half. Chop
up some sweet pickle or use pimientos to dress the top of each.
Refrigerate.

Southern Potato Salad

When anyone in the South is in trouble, a true Southern Belle will take over potato salad, because down here in the South, it is the ultimate comfort food.

> 2 cans potato slices, drained
> 6 boiled eggs, chopped
> 1 onion, chopped
> 2 tablespoons sweet pickle relish
> 1 tablespoon mustard
> 2 tablespoons mayonnaise
> ½ teaspoon celery seed

1. Mix all ingredients in a bowl.

2. Arrange washed and dried lettuce leaves on a platter, then place the potato salad on top of the lettuce leaves.

3. Sprinkle paprika over the top of the potato salad, and refrigerate covered until served.

Cole Slaw

If you are gonna have a bar-b-q, you'd better have an incredible homemade cole slaw to go with it.

> 1 head cabbage (or package of pre-shredded cabbage)
> 1 large carrot
> ½ cup real mayonnaise
> 1 teaspoon salt
> 1 teaspoon pepper
> 1 teaspoon sugar (optional)

1. Buy a package of shredded cabbage or shred a head cabbage into a large bowl. Shred the carrot into this.

2. Add the mayonnaise, salt, pepper, and sugar (if desired). Mix well.

3. Cover and chill until time to serve.

Fried Squash

Southerners will eat anything that is fried. I mean, think about it, squash?!

1 medium yellow summer squash, cut into ¼-inch-
thick slices
1 egg
½ cup milk
½ cup vegetable oil
1 cup self-rising cornmeal
Salt
Pepper

1. Wash your yellow summer squash and cut off both ends. Cut into ¼-inch-thick slices (about like a tomato slice).

2. In one dish beat together the egg and the milk. In another dish place the cornmeal. In a skillet, heat the vegetable oil to 375°F.

3. Dip each slice of squash into the egg-milk mixture, then in the cornmeal. Lay each slice carefully in the hot oil.

4. When one side is golden brown, flip it over and let the other side fry golden brown. They cook fast.

5. Drain on paper towels. Season with salt and pepper as desired.

Fried Okra

Again, I tell you, who wouldn't love fried okra—it is *fried*!

> 2 pounds fresh okra, cut into ½-inch-thick slices
> 6 cups oil, for frying
> ½ cup cornmeal
> 1 cup all-purpose flour
> 1 teaspoon salt
> ½ teaspoon black pepper
> ½ teaspoon garlic powder
> ¼ teaspoon cayenne pepper
> ½ cup buttermilk

1. Wash the okra and cut it into ½-inch-thick slices.

2. Heat the oil in a large, heavy-bottomed skillet or Dutch oven to 350 degrees F. (You may not need to use this much oil; do not fill the pan more than halfway up the sides with oil.)

3. In a medium bowl, combine cornmeal, flour, salt, black pepper, garlic powder, and cayenne pepper.

4. Dip each okra slice in buttermilk, then dredge in the cornmeal-flour mixture to coat well.

5. Carefully add okra to the hot oil and cook until golden brown. (It may be necessary to fry the okra in batches.)

6. Remove from oil, drain on paper towels, and serve immediately.

Fried Green Tomatoes

The movie made this recipe famous—believe it or not, fried green tomatoes are yum, yum, yum!

> **3 medium, firm green tomatoes**
> **½ teaspoon salt**
> **¼ teaspoon pepper**
> **½ cup all-purpose flour**
> **¼ cup milk**
> **2 eggs, beaten**
> **⅔ cup fine dry bread crumbs or cornmeal**
> **¼ cup olive oil**

1. Cut unpeeled tomatoes into ½-inch-thick slices. Sprinkle slices with salt and pepper, and let them stand for 15 minutes.

2. Meanwhile, place flour, milk, eggs, and bread crumbs in four separate shallow dishes.

3. Heat 2 tablespoons of olive oil in a skillet over medium heat.

4. Dip tomato slices in milk, then flour, then eggs, then bread crumbs.

5. In the skillet, fry half of the coated tomato slices at a time, for 4–6 minutes on each side or until brown. As you cook the rest of the tomatoes, add olive oil as needed.

6. Season to taste with salt and pepper.

Collard Greens

Okay, I must tell you, I cannot stand collard greens. However, that doesn't mean my man doesn't love them, and what he loves, I should cook!

½ pound smoked meat (ham hocks, smoked turkey wings, or smoked neck bones)
½ teaspoon salt
¼ teaspoon black pepper
¼ teaspoon garlic powder
1 tablespoon seasoned salt
1 tablespoon hot red pepper sauce
1 large bunch collard greens
1 tablespoon butter

1. In a large pot, bring 3 quarts of water to a boil and add smoked meat, salt, black pepper, garlic powder, seasoned salt, and hot sauce. Reduce heat to medium and cook for 1 hour.

2. Wash the collard greens thoroughly. Remove the stems that run down the center by holding the leaf in your left hand and stripping the leaf down with your right hand. The tender young leaves in the heart of the collards don't need to be stripped.

3. Stack 6 to 8 leaves, roll up, and slice into ½- to 1-inch thick slices.

4. Place greens in the pot with meat and add the butter. Cook 45 to 60 minutes, stirring occasionally, until tender. When done, taste and adjust seasoning.

Southern Fried Chicken

I love, love, love fried chicken, and no man I've ever dated has turned it down. In fact, anything fried is a man magnet in the food world down here. Every Southern woman has her own recipe that turns a regular ol' chicken into a crispy, brown, juicy delight. When frying, you need a big ol' frying pan with a lot, I repeat, a lot of oil in it. Still others use a deep-fryer, but, no matter what your method, you still need a bunch of that oil. It's a messy dish to fix, but well worth it, especially when your man sits down and eats it all!

I'd like to be able to offer this recipe in the traditional way, with specific measurements, but no one does her chicken that way. It's just not natural! It's a trial-and-error method, but I can tell you that it's very simple.

> **1 whole fryer chicken, cut into pieces**
> **All-purpose flour**
> **Buttermilk**
> **Salt and pepper**
> **Vegetable or canola oil (not olive oil or anything fancy)**

1. Get out two bowls—put all-purpose flour (maybe 2 cups) into one bowl, with a little salt and pepper mixed in, and put the buttermilk (about 2 cups) in the other.

2. Pour the oil into your skillet until it is about one-third full. Heat the oil on medium to low-high heat. Your oil is ready to use when you sprinkle a little water from your hands onto it and the water dances off the oil.

3. Wash and pat dry your chicken pieces. Put a piece of chicken into the flour, and coat it well. Then dip it in the buttermilk, coating it. Dip it one last time in the flour, then set it in the hot oil. Do this with as many pieces that will comfortably fit into your skillet at one time.

4. Your chicken will begin to brown on one side and you'll need to turn it over so the other side can get cooked. I can't tell you how long to cook the chicken because it varies with the size, the stove, etc. If it is golden brown on the outside, I'd suggest pulling a bigger piece from the skillet, and cutting into it. If the bigger one is done, then the little ones are as well. Again, it's a trial-and-error process, but well worth the effort.

6. Drain the chicken on a paper towel before serving, to get rid of any excess grease. Serve it up hot!

Easy Chicken and Dumplings

Everybody loves chicken and dumplings around here, but it is hard as hell to make if you are a busy Southern belle. Here is a recipe that takes shortcuts but is still yummy!

> **1 can cream of chicken soup**
> **2 cups heavy cream**
> **½ stick butter**
> **2 cans refrigerated biscuits**
> **Salt and pepper to taste**

1. In a large pot, combine the soup and cream over medium heat until smooth. Add the butter and seasonings. Heat until it comes to a boil, but don't let it stick.

2. Pinch off bite-size pieces of the biscuit dough and drop carefully into the hot liquid.

3. When all the dough is in the pot, cover and let the mixture simmer for 10 minutes without stirring. After 10 minutes, stir the mixture and let simmer 5 more minutes. Serve hot.

Meatloaf

Every man, I promise you, loves meatloaf. Try this one, and you will have him salivatin' in no time!

> 2 pounds ground sirloin, turkey, or pork
> 3 cups dry oats
> 2 eggs, beaten
> ½ cup chopped onions or 2 tsp. onion powder
> ½ teaspoon celery seeds
> 1 can sliced carrots, drained and mashed
> 1 can tomato soup
> 2 teaspoons dry mustard
> 3 tablespoons brown sugar
> ½ cup ketchup
> 1 teaspoon dry mustard

1. Preheat oven to 350°F.

2. In a bowl mix all the ingredients except the brown sugar, ketchup, and mustard. Pour mixture into a loaf pan.

3. Before you put the loaf in the oven, mix together the brown sugar, ketchup, and mustard, and coat the top with the mixture.

4. Bake about one hour, until meat is thoroughly cooked.

Fried Pork Chops

Yeah, Southern men like their meats, so this is a winner!

> **6 cups vegetable oil**
> **1 teaspoon of salt**
> **½ teaspoon teaspoon black pepper**
> **½ teaspoon garlic powder**
> **½ teaspoon seasoned salt**
> **6 pork chops**
> **1 cup buttermilk**
> **1 cup all-purpose flour**

1. Heat oil in a large, heavy-bottomed pot to 350°F.

2. Sprinkle some of the salt, pepper, garlic powder, and seasoned salt on both sides of the pork chops, rubbing them thoroughly into the meat.

3. Pour buttermilk over meat, and turn to coat on all sides.

4. Season the flour generously with salt, pepper, and garlic powder, then roll each chop into flour, and shake off the excess.

5. Carefully place the chops, two at a time, into the hot oil, and cook until the outside is golden brown. Take one chop out and make a small cut at the thickest part to test for doneness; adjust time accordingly for the rest.

6. Drain on paper towels before serving.

Pigs in Blankets

This is a great thing to have before a Super Bowl party, or for a casual main course.

> 1 pound of cocktail sausage
> 1 can refrigerated biscuits
> 1 pound cheese
> 3 tablespoons margarine, melted

1. Preheat oven to 375°F.

2. Make lengthwise slits in sausages. Cut cheese into strips small enough to put into slits in sausage.

3. Quarter each biscuit, and shape into a spiral around each cheese stuffed sausage. Brush biscuit with melted margarine.

4. Bake until biscuits are browned, about 10–12 minutes.

Miss Irene's Dinner Rolls

We were raised on homemade rolls, biscuits, and corn bread. You can eat them with anything. My favorite way is to eat the rolls and biscuits with just a big jar of honey and jelly, and with a big hunk of butter. For really good corn bread, butter is all that's needed. My old boyfriend wouldn't eat vegetables unless he had a roll or square of corn bread to go along with them. Men love meat and bread, so you're pretty much always going to score if you can master one of these recipes. My favorite rolls in the world were made by the cook my mama had as a child. Miss Irene made these rolls every single day and nothing beat their scrumptious, light taste.

1 cup warm water
2¼ teaspoons active dry yeast
¼ cup sugar
¼ cup butter, melted and cooled, or softened
1 egg, well beaten
1 tablespoon salt
3 cups all-purpose flour

1. Preheat the oven to 375°F.

2. Put the water in a mixing bowl and add the yeast, sugar, butter, egg, and salt. Then add your flour and mix well with a fork.

3. Knead it (fold dough over and press lightly with the heel of your hand) on a lightly floured surface for about 3 minutes. Put the dough in the refrigerator for an hour, uncovered.

4. Shape your rolls any way you want (Miss Irene just made a basic shape) and let them rise uncovered until about doubled in size.

5. Bake at 375°F until lightly browned on top. You can brush the tops with butter if desired.

Mayonnaise Rolls

If that recipe looks too daunting, here's an easy one that doesn't require all that kneading and rising.

> **1 cup self-rising flour**
> **1 tablespoon sugar**
> **½ cup milk**
> **1 tablespoon mayonnaise**

Combine all the ingredients and cook in greased muffin tins at 400°F until golden brown. See? I told you this one would be easy!

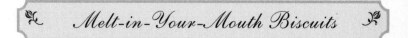

Melt-in-Your-Mouth Biscuits

Have you ever had a biscuit that was so light, flaky, and moist that you didn't even need butter? These are fabulous, with or without butter. If you serve them up with a jar of honey or jelly, you can make a complete meal out of them. Or try them with Southern Style Chocolate Gravy (p. 163) for a real treat!

> 2 cups all-purpose flour
> 1 tablespoon baking powder
> 2 teaspoons sugar
> 1 teaspoon salt
> ⅓ cup solid vegetable shortening
> ⅔ cup whole milk

1. Preheat the oven to 450°F.

2. Sift the dry ingredients into a mixing bowl.

3. Cut the shortening into the flour mixture with a pastry blender, two knives, or blending fork, until the mixture looks like meal.

4. Stir in almost all the milk. If the dough does not seem pliable, add the remaining milk—use enough milk to make a soft, puffy dough that will be easy to roll out.

5. Knead the dough on a lightly floured surface. Too much handling makes tough biscuits. Roll or pat out the dough ¼-inch thick for thin, crusty biscuits or ½-inch thick for thick, soft biscuits. Each biscuit should be 1–2 inches in diameter.

6. Place on ungreased cookie sheet, close together to have biscuits with soft sides, or an inch apart for biscuits with crusty sides. Bake for 10 to 12 minutes at 450°F.

Slap Your Mama Corn Bread

There's hardly nothing more Southern than corn bread. We can eat it with just about anything! My favorite memory was of my grandfather's cook, Miss Irene. She made her buttery, sweet corn bread in a cast-iron corn bread mold. The smell of it cooking was enough to make you swoon. Then, she serve it to us with piles of butter. I didn't think there was anything better on this earth! It's so good, as the saying goes, "It'll make you wanna slap your mama!"

⅔ cup vegetable or canola oil

2 eggs

> 2½ cups milk
> 2 cups cornmeal
> 2 cups all-pupose flour
> 2 tablespoons baking powder
> 1 tablespoon baking soda
> 1 teaspoon salt

1. Preheat the oven to 475°F.

2. Put the oil in a bowl and add the eggs. Beat the mixture until it's foamy.

3. Add the milk and sift in the dry ingredients.

4. Pour the mixture into a greased 8-inch-square cake pan or a muffin pan and bake at 475°F for 20 minutes.

Chess Piiiiiiie

Chess "piiiiiiie" (you gotta say it right) is a Southern delicacy that is completely bad for you if you are watching your weight, cholesterol, or sugar intake—hell, it's bad for you even if you're healthy and fit as a horse. Why? It's basically made from sugar, butter, and eggs. No man can resist it. Its texture is smooth, and the taste is sweet, sweet, sweet. Men love dessert and the praise you receive from baking this will be plentiful. If chess piiiiiiie doesn't sound that good to you, I'll show you how to make banana pud-din' so you'll have another good recipe to have in your pretty little recipe box.

> 5 egg yolks
> 1¾ cups sugar
> 1 heaping tablespoon cornmeal
> 1 heaping tablespoon all-purpose flour
> ½ cup butter, melted
> 1 cup whole milk
> 2 teaspoons vanilla extract
> 1 unbaked pie shell

1. Preheat the oven to 350°F.

2. Beat egg yolks with 1 cup of the sugar until light.

3. In another bowl, mix the remaining ¾ cup of sugar with the flour and cornmeal.

4. Combine the two mixtures and flavor with the vanilla.

5. Pour into the unbaked pie shell and bake at 350°F for about an hour, until the filling is set. It is set when you can shake the pie gently and the center is firm. Serve warm or cool, and top with whipped cream if you'd like.

Banana Puddin' from Scratch

Banana puddin' is a Southern classic and is yummy. You can either follow the recipe below or you can always refer to the recipe printed on the side of the Nilla Wafer box!

> **1 cup sugar**
> **3 eggs, beaten**
> **1 dash salt**
> **2 tablespoons cornstarch**
> **2 cups whole milk**
> **1 teaspoon vanilla extract**
> **3–4 ripe bananas, sliced**
> **Vanilla wafers**

1. Mix together the sugar and eggs.

2. Add the salt, cornstarch, and milk.

3. Bring the mixture to a boil over medium-high heat until it is thickened. Be sure to stir often to prevent it from sticking to the pan.

4. Remove from the heat and add the vanilla, mixing well. Layer the wafers, bananas, and pudding. Top with more wafers.

No-Bake Chocolate Oatmeal Cookies

If you ain't much of a cook, this is a super way to give your man home baked cookies without having to *really* cook them!

> 2 cups sugar
> ½ cup peanut butter
> ½ cup milk
> 2½ cups oatmeal
> ⅓ cup cocoa
> 1 teaspoon vanilla
> 1 stick margarine

1. Mix sugar, peanut butter, milk, oatmeal, and cocoa in a saucepan. Bring to a boil, and cook for 1 minute while stirring constantly.

2. Add vanilla and margarine, and mix well.

3. Drop by tablespoons onto foil; allow to harden.

Peanut Brittle

Every Southern belle knows the value of having a good peanut brittle recipe under her belt. Who can resist that buttery, crunchy, salty goodness?

2 teaspoons margarine

2 cups raw peanuts

2 cups white Karo syrup

2 cups sugar

¼ teaspoon salt

1 tablespoon baking soda

1. Grease a cookie sheet with margarine.

2. Combine peanuts, syrup, sugar, and salt in a heavy saucepan. Bring to a rolling boil. Cook until golden brown and the peanuts pop, or 285 degrees on candy thermometer.

3. Stir in baking soda and mix quickly.

4. Pour onto the prepared cookie sheet. Let cool and break into pieces.

Southern-Style Chocolate Gravy

Oh my God! This is something you should try even if you are grossed out by the title of the recipe. Trust me!

2 tablespoons cocoa

1¼ cups sugar

2 tablespoons cornstarch

2 cups milk

1. Mix cocoa, sugar, and cornstarch in a 2-quart saucepan. Gradually stir in the 2 cups of milk.

2. When thoroughly mixed, cook over medium heat, stirring often to prevent scorching, until thickened.

3. Remove from heat and serve with hot biscuits.

Sweet Iiiiced Tea

Sweet iiiiced tea (another important pronunciation) flows through the veins of most Southerners. You might be saying that iiiiced tea doesn't sound that unique, but aaaah, the way we do it down here is so different. I swear I think the goal is to make it taste more like sugar than tea. It is the sweetest liquid you'll put in your mouth, if you follow the traditional recipe. But I gotta tell you, men love their iiiiced tea, too, and they never complain about its very sugary taste. But be aware, that ever since the Northern influence that arrived after the War of Northern Aggression (that's what some call the Civil War down here), it has become somewhat acceptable to drink unsweetened iced tea. So if you're touring down here, you need to know that when waitress looks at you and asks "sweetie?" she's not trying to make a play for you—she just wants to know if you want your tea sweet.

You may be thinking that sweet iiiiced tea is made by putting sugar in your tea, but you'd be wrong. The sugar is added while the tea is boiling on the stove. The process is simple, really:

1. Take as many tea bags as you want for the quantity you'll be using, and make the tea per the instructions.

2. As the tea is boiling, add lots of sugar. How much? Down here there's no such thing. Just add it to taste until you can taste at least as much sugar as the tea. Add a little more sugar after that, if you're brave!

3. After the sugar is completely melted, you can either let the concoction cool or pour it directly over ice. Garnish with lemon or a sprig, of mint if you'd like.

So now you have a full arsenal of qualities and foods that convey hospitality to men. If these recipes don't wet your whistle, you can't go wrong by checking out any Junior League cookbook published in the South. I promise you that if you follow even a fourth of what you've read in this chapter, no man will be immune from your bewitching ways!

Top 5 Things a Southern Belle Should Never Serve a Man

1 Quiche

2 Crepes

3 Spinach salad

4 Fondue

5 Anything he can't easily pronounce

CHAPTER EIGHT

Why Buy the Cow . . . ?

A woman's dress should be like a barbed-wire fence: serving its purpose without obstructing the view.

—Sophia Loren

While many of us have been known to give it away in exchange for a commitment, or better yet, jewelry, still others use sex as a "prize" for a man who treats them right! Everyone knows that a good Southern belle is *supposed* to remain chaste and pristine, but sometimes what has been known to happen in the backseat of that Buick is just too tempting! There are no judgments here about whether you should or shouldn't have sex before marriage, or how soon is too soon to embark on a sexual relationship. You have to figure that one out for yourself. All I *can* tell you is that we Southern belles know how to use our sexuality, and we also know some things that the rest of you don't. So let's get down to business.

But first, we'd better get the virginity issue out in the open. Many people who aren't from the South think we are virgins until we get married, being that we are in the Bible Belt and all. Don't want to burst anyone's bubble, but I gotta be honest with you. Southern belles *really do* have sex before marriage. I can hear the gasps as you read this, but yep, shocking as it is for you, it is true.

But here's where we differ from women from other parts of the country: we simply reinvent our virginity when the situation calls for it. Sounds crazy, doesn't it? It would be, except for the fact that we are known as ladies who pride ourselves on being mannerly and having good morals. But we are also human, so when we catch ourselves in a situation that later on we tell ourselves was a mistake, we can manipulate the facts so that the little tiaras on our heads don't become tarnished! With sex, it goes something like this:

It (sex) didn't count if:

- ✿ All your clothes were on
- ✿ You were in the backseat of a car, truck, or van
- ✿ You were in the water
- ✿ All the lights were on
- ✿ You couldn't remember his last name
- ✿ You didn't speak the same language
- ✿ You weren't wearing lipstick
- ✿ You were wearing "laundry day" panties
- ✿ You were wearing your tiara
- ✿ He left his hat or socks on
- ✿ You were wearing your little blue "Monica" dress

The point is simple: Pretending that "it didn't count" is a marvelous way to tell your man that you're either still a virgin or that you haven't had nearly as much experience as you have, which everyone knows intimidates a man!

Is there a difference between foreplay versus teasing versus playing hard to get? Men will tell you that teasing is what we girls do that get them all hot and bothered, but that we have no plans to take it further. Foreplay, they will explain, gives the guy a glimmer of hope that sex will actually take place. Playing hard to get is just plain silly, they say. Now given that they are, after all, only men, and they think so much of the time with their penises, I think I will have to weigh in and offer my expert opinion.

Teasing

Teasing is a precursor to foreplay. It's that innocent batting of the eyes, the touch on the leg, and the provocative way you run your hand across your chest. This indicates that you are having fun and wouldn't mind seeing if things could go further. You use teasing to let a guy know it's okay for him to move forward, if you know what I mean.

Foreplay

If the teasing is going well, you will then move into the foreplay portion of the evening. The touching gets more personal, and there may be kissing. My stepdaughter calls it "the trip to the petting zoo." Now I warn you that if you engage in such behavior, be very careful about the message you are sending. Since most translate these acts into the assumption that sex will follow, you need to be on your game. If you don't want to have sex, either don't go this far or make it clear that you have no intentions of going further.

You certainly wouldn't want to send the wrong message and be known as the girl who always "plays hard to get."

Playing Hard to Get

Playing hard to get is a mixed message. If you really think about it, your body tells you that you are attracted to someone, not your mind. Some women play hard to get because they are so uncomfortable in such situations. This is their way to get attention but keep things from getting out of hand (or *in hand*, as the case may be!). On the other hand, some women use playing hard to get as a form of teasing to determine *if* they have any intention of going home with a man.

My husband and other so-called male experts tell me that you can only do the teasing/playing-hard-to-get thing once or twice with the same guy because if there's an alternative (i.e., another woman), he'll go elsewhere. And although we hate to admit he's right, he's got a point. Men just don't like to go fishing where the fish ain't biting!

Teasing, foreplay, playing hard to get. Call it what you want, but understand that while these behaviors can have men drooling all over you, they can also be misinterpreted so easily that things can go in a different direction in the blink of an eye. Southern belles know what they are doing and what they want, but they never wish to cause undue embarrassment or discomfort to themselves and others!

SEXY SECRETS THAT ALL SOUTHERN BELLES KNOW

Now, let's face it, there's plenty we don't know about men not because they are complicated, but because there's lots of stuff we don't *care* to know. When it comes to sex, though, Southern belles have some inside knowledge that must be passed on to the rest of you.

1. Men are almost always insecure about their performance, particularly in this day and age. Think about it. If he is pretty sure he isn't your first, the competitive nature in a man automatically pops out. He will want to know what you think about him standing naked in front of you. Now, if I were you, Miss Priss, I'd resist the urge to laugh out loud or make any other gesture that suggests he isn't anything special. He'll just shrivel up, excuse the pun, if he feels inferior in any way. You don't have to go all gaga over him, particularly if the sex wasn't that good. If you do, then he'll think you want more, and then you are really stuck! But you don't have to be mean, either. Find yourself a balance. If he was the best you've ever had, or at least in a long time, he will love to hear how he made your toes curl! We love men, but they *do* require quite a bit of ego-boosting and if you've read this book thus far, you know how to do that!

2. Men are intimidated if you know more in the bedroom than they do. It's funny. Even though he may find the things you *do* fun and fascinating, that competition gene kicks in again. All of a sudden, the fact that you are more experienced or knowledgeable gets translated into, "Oh, she's been around the block quite a few times." All of a sudden, you are no longer Miss Southern Vixen, you are now Miss Southern Trash. Hey, I'm not saying it's fair, but it *does* happen. So don't use all your "tricks" right away. Keep him guessing, and let him be the one to know more every once in a while. You'll still know the truth. But if there is some "trick" that you feel you simply must use, you can always say you read about it in *Cosmo* or in a novel. Men will always fall for that.

3.   **For a Southern girl, having sex with a man means "I might love you" at the very least.** For any man, sex means "I like you enough to have sex with you," or "I'll do it with anybody if they show an interest." Southern belles like sex, but they have feelings and emotions attached to it. They believe that the person they are contemplating having sex with is a potential keeper. Yet they also understand that if they choose to have sex with someone they like, it may not hold the same meaning for him. Thus, Southern women know to be choosy about how and when to have sex because it can create all sorts of complications. (A one-night stand is a whole different matter, and the modern Southern girl is not a stranger to this activity. Think "it doesn't count if . . .")

4.   **Okay, this will get your attention. A lot of men actually groom themselves <u>down there</u>!** Yep, you read it here. My friend,

Ben, explained that things can get sort of murky and difficult to navigate *down there* and that women actually appreciate a guy who takes the time to tidy things up a bit. He warned that we shouldn't find this behavior odd or weird; rather we ought to bestow our gratitude on any man who is willing to do what it takes to keep a situation from becoming too hairy!

5.   When guys get together, the subject of sex inevitably comes up, especially if they are drinking. You know this already. What you don't know is that men don't always kiss and tell. If you embark on a one-night stand, you will almost always become a topic of conversation. If he respects you or has feelings for you, he will keep the graphic details to himself. He might imply that you are the best he's ever had, but he will not say anything that would cause his pals to snicker when you are around. A lot of women get their panties in a wad if they know men have talked about them in *that way*. Southern women understand that boys will be boys, and that they just can't help themselves when it comes to sex. Therefore, they know to be careful whom they "lay up with" if they don't want to get a reputation or be the topic at the next "boys' night out!"

6.   Get this. There are days when men <u>actually don't</u> want to have sex. When I made this announcement in front of Ben, his eyes widened and his jaw dropped. "I'd have to be bleeding from two orifices before I would refuse sex!" I checked around in case I was wrong. No, other guys confirmed that while those days are few and far between, it does happen. They don't like us to know about it because it somehow hurts their manly pride. Physical exhaustion, sickness, and too much stress top the list as the reasons they may refuse us. Don't take it personally if he isn't in the mood. Accept his reasons graciously and then do your best to cheer him up. As soon as you do, he'll be back in the saddle again, ready to ride!

Even when he's in a relationship, he will still masturbate—often. Michelle and I were at a favorite watering hole one night and she was helping me with this chapter. Two guys we knew, who will remain unnamed, were there—a bartender and a manager. One was in a relationship and one was single. The question was how often a man masturbates in a week. Then we argued about which day of the week starts the actual week, but that's another story. Michelle and I ventured that once a day should be plenty. They laughed in our faces. The single guy responded, "Okay, this is Wednesday, so let's look between Sunday up through today." Yes? "About 18 times." Umm, let's see, 18 divided by 4 equals 4.2. Really? He nodded proudly. The guy in a relationship said on a weekly basis, about six times. This confirms what all women need to realize about men. It's not that we aren't attractive enough, or sexy enough, or that we put out enough. The bottom line is, as Ben put it, "You'd play with it, too, if you had one." Men like their penises almost as much as they like us!

7. **Men like sex—duh.** They like it sleazy and they like it sweet. They need to be in control over what is happening but

many women consider this Neanderthal-ish and so don't want to participate. What Southern women know, though, is that the control they have is simply an illusion. We allow them to think they have control because it makes them feel good about themselves. They take their cues from us, and then they try to set the pace. For example, if you'd rather him touch you "there," gently take his hand and put it where you want it. Then coo about how he knows just what you like. This is a simple gesture that hurts no one. He gets to feel as if he's king of the jungle and you get to have fun. What's wrong with that?

8. **Men do not expect you to guess what they like in bed, but they sure as hell aren't going to say anything unless you ask.** Southern women have a way of doing this that is subtle, never humiliating, and pretty effective. It entails using our most sugary voices along with gentle touches and simple questions. "How's that, sugah?" Or, "does that feel niiice?" You get the picture, don't you? Demanding to know what he likes or wants puts him on the spot in more ways than one. Instead of, "What position do you prefer?" a sultry "How do you *want* me?" is much more effective. The object is to please him, not to scare him!

Be Prepared

Girls, it's the twenty-first century. Do not assume that every man carries around a condom in his wallet. You must be prepared. No self-respecting Southern girl says, "Why, I would never keep those things around." She doesn't flaunt them either, but she is ready "just in case." This does not make you a slut, it makes you smart.

I once knew a girl who always carried what she called her "possibles bag." It was about the size of a cosmetic case that would fit in a reasonably sized pocketbook. Her "possibles bag" contained items like a lipstick, a tampon, a wet wipe in a foil packet, breath mints, a twenty-dollar bill, a sample-size perfume, *and* a condom (also in a foil packet). This Southern belle could handle just about any minor emergency without embarrassment . . . unless she mixed up the foil packets!

Pre-Sex Buzz Kills

Even the best-bred Southern girl slips up now and then, so we all need to be reminded that there are certain things that are best kept to yourself if you don't want to kill the moment. Let's talk for a minute about what *not* to say before you have sex. As you know by now, Southern belles are big on manners.

1. **"Your penis is soooooo cute!"** I know some of you are thinking that this sounds sweet. Well, in fact, I guess it does, but are you really going for sweet at that moment? I didn't think so.

If you must comment on his size, there are far better ways to do it. How about the tried and true Southern way? "Well, well, well, look at that!" Or, "Well, hello *there!*" Personally, I just have never felt like saying anything about a guy's penis, except for once. I dated a guy once whose penis was bent and pointed sharply to the left. I was intrigued, and though I didn't mean to, I could not stop staring. Now that would have been fine because this particular man was quite arrogant and probably thought I was impressed. The problem was that I could not stop giggling and making corny jokes like, "Whoa, where's he headed?" It did not help the situation one bit.

2. **"I shouldn't have had all that bean dip."** You might have just had the best Mexican dinner ever, but no one, absolutely no one, wants to hear about it. This is especially true if you are preparing to have sex. Now I'm not sure what to tell you if you really *do* have the urge to pass a good bit of gas. I guess my first thought would be that you might wanna pass, pardon the pun, on the sex. But if you're a gal who has incredible control over this problem, and you can hold it in, more power to you. If you are the type who knows how to do it in a silent, subtle way, go ahead. I simply don't have that sort of confidence.

3. **"Do you believe in love at first sight?"** If you want to frighten the hell out of a man, ask that right before you have sex. Nothing will kill the mood faster. Look, you don't know what's going to happen when you have sex, and *you* be may the one who can't wait to get out of there. It's better that you leave yourself with some choices. The intent is not to scare him, but to enjoy being with him.

4. **"We'll have to keep our voices down. My parents are asleep in the next room."** You may be asking why you'd even consider

having sex with a guy when you live with your parents, but I ask *you*, did you see *Failure to Launch*? Okay then, don't be so quick to judge. All I'm saying is you might want to have an alternative spot to do the deed so you don't have to meet his parents that soon! Unlike the mother in the movie, I don't know any mamas who would find anything funny about stepping into the hall to find a strange young lady making her way to the bathroom. Awkward! It's not a great way to begin a relationship!

5. **"I just got over a nasty case of crabs."** Talk about your buzz-kill! I'm not suggesting that you shouldn't be mindful of any "conditions" you might have *down there*, but the time to mention it is not right before sex. Hopefully you know this already, but like a friend of mine said, "Don't we say the dumbest things at the worst moments?" She's right in that we let things slip out that are better kept to ourselves, or at least discussed at another time. I guess my best advice here is to clear up whatever you've got going on and don't even consider going near a man until you do!

In-the-Middle-of-Sex Buzz Kills

What about things you shouldn't say or do *during* sex?

1. **First and foremost, if you have another man's name on your mind, just keep your mouth shut.** Don't make the mistake of calling out your old boyfriend's name in a fit of passion. It'll kill the moment, and to be honest, it's just bad manners.

2. If your cell phone rings, don't answer it. It rang when my pal MK was having sex with her own Dr. McDreamy. She just *had* to take the call, and just her luck, it was her old boyfriend, Luke. She wasn't quite over him, so she used her current situation to rub it in Luke's face. Needless to say, McDreamy wasn't amused.

3. If you are unfortunate enough to be having the worst sex ever, there's no need to contribute by making monotone noises clearly communicating your disappointment and boredom. If he's the gentlemanly type and wants you to "go first," this *would* be one of the few times to fake an orgasm. But keep it low-key, so he won't wonder why he's not getting another date! It won't last forever, and you don't have to do it again if you don't want.

4. I don't care what you say, there is nothing interesting about the ceiling, so don't stare at it while you're having sex. Give your man your undivided attention—you can think about other stuff later. And need I even bring up yawning, falling asleep, or passing out? All no-nos, and all equally offensive.

5. Fight the temptation to talk dirty unless you are absolutely sure you have a receptive audience. Not everyone finds talking dirty an erotic turn-on. Take my friend MK. Her prowess for dirty talk was legendary among her friends and past suitors. She was having sex for the first time with a man she'd had a huge crush on, and in the middle, she started saying things that would make most Southern belles blush. Her date began laughing and couldn't stop. Finally, when he caught his breath, he told her that she was the funniest girl he'd ever met, but she'd have to shut up because he couldn't stop laughing. MK was insulted because she was positive that he was finding her running commentary to be the perfect aphrodisiac! At least this time, she was dead wrong.

6.   **If you don't want to have sex with a man, find a way to say "no thanks."** Rejection is bad enough—you don't have to be mean. Here are some that I have been told work perfectly while keeping a man's dignity in check.

- ❀   "Dahlin', I'd love to, but my 'Aunt Flo' is visiting. Can I have a rain check?" Yep, that oughta do it!
- ❀   "You know I'd love to, but I have to get up early tomorrow for Sunday school." It's a perfect Saturday-night excuse.
- ❀   "I'd love to have sex with you! I'm ovulating, and you'd make the best daddy!" Need I say more?
- ❀   "I've had a lot to drink and I'm sick to my stomach." No man really wants to nurse you while you're paying homage to the "porcelain princess."
- ❀   "I'd rather wait 'til I get to know you better." He'll either run because he doesn't want any commitment, or he'll respect you and not push.
- ❀   "No, I'd rather not."

Just remember, you *are* in control and *no* really *does* mean *no*! Saying no the Southern belle way is not only kind, but it also leaves the door open in case you change your mind.

7.   Don't rush through undressing. As you have now discovered, Southern belles know how to dress. If you think you are going to have sex, understand that the taking off of your clothes is part of foreplay. Try turning your back to your beau and seductively slip your bra strap from your shoulder. Ask him to unzip your dress. Men find that incredibly erotic!

8.   There are several articles of clothing that are <u>never</u> sexy. Lose the eighteen-hour bra and white granny panties, at least for the night. Don't wear clothing that is hard to remove. If you have trouble with it, a man will find it impossible. Socks, especially if you've had them on a while, don't cut it in the sexy department. No matter how you do it, you cannot peel those suckers off in a way that turns a man on! If you don't believe me, try it.

9.   Remember your hygiene. Scented candles do not cover up all odors, so need I say more? Likewise, stubbly legs are not sexy.

10.   Don't use alcohol to make yourself more uninhibited. No matter how limber and relaxed you think it will make you, you won't be nearly as sexy and graceful as you believe. And you'll probably just end up making an ass of yourself!

11. Never, ever, never apologize for your body. Don't let your worries about dimples, pimples, sags, or bags stop you from enjoying yourself. There's nothing men find more attractive and sexy than a confident, self-assured woman who is not self-conscious about these things.

A chapter about what Southern belles know about sex wouldn't be complete without the subject of naming penises. There's an old joke among women that asks why men name their penises. It's because they don't want a perfect stranger making all their important decisions! Actually, it is very convenient for a man's penis to have a name, because we all know that Southern belles love euphemisms. Good gracious, it is just so embarrassing and direct to say "penis"! And, it makes it so much easier to talk about sex. Instead of the very stilted, "Are you interested in having sex now?" the Southern belle can ask, "Sugah, can Big Baby come out and play?" See, how much better that is? So yes, naming the penis is important. Personally, I think a man who has *not* named his penis might seriously be lacking in a sense of humor, and no Southern belle wants a man who cannot laugh at himself.

So if it doesn't have a name, perhaps it will be up to you to christen it, so to speak. Now, how do you come up with the perfect name? Imagine saying "I sure would like to play with Percival." Who wants to play with Percival? No, it has to be a manly or funny name. If your guy's penis has a geeky name, his penis is probably geeky, too. Maybe it wears thick glasses and white socks. Unfortunately, you probably find that out *before* you find out the pet name! The cool thing is, if you don't like your man's penis name, you can always give it a new one!

My friend Mary Jane knew a guy in college named John. He stood at five foot six, was skinny as a rail, had early-onset balding, had a wicked sense of humor, and was cute as a button. Though John was shorter than average, he was a ladykiller and his charms were legendary. John called his penis "Little Elvis." Judging by the way girls swooned over him, one can only guess that "little" was not really the proper adjective. Anyway, John's buddies used to laugh, "John and Little Elvis are on the prowl tonight!"

For the guys who were honest enough to answer my question "Does your penis have a name?" I thank you. You are all courageous, funny, and awfully proud of yourselves, aren't you? Here are but a few that I can print here:

- ✿ "Big Daddy" (okay, a little weird, but I can see where it might work)
- ✿ "Tex" (he is from Texas)
- ✿ "Blue Ribbon" (as in "I am the best prize in the world!")
- ✿ "Soldier" (as in, "Salute!")
- ✿ "Rocky" (do I really need to explain?)
- ✿ "Pokey" (hmmm . . . maybe a little low in self-esteem, but sort of cute)
- ✿ "Cupcake" (sweet, sweet, sweet)
- ✿ "Uncle Louie" (this may be the oddest since this particular guy actually had an uncle named, you got it, Louie!)
- ✿ "Mister Happy" (lacking in originality, but it'll do)

- "Stanley" (as in Stanley Power Tools)
- "Eddy" (The guy's name is Ed, so he and his penis are known as Ed and Eddy!)
- "Mr. Lonely" (for the poorly pathetic man who isn't getting any!)

Get with your girlfriends and fill in the space below with your favorites!

———————————————————————

———————————————————————

———————————————————————

———————————————————————

So there you have it. Sex can be fun, it can be serious, or it doesn't have to happen at all! You make the choice that's best for you, and don't let anyone tell you any different! You'll do good to remember what any self-respectin' Southern belle would when it comes to sex: Kiss if you wish, be careful who you tell, for a good reputation will always serve you well!

Top 5 Times a Southern Belle Won't Find Her Man Romantic

1 Around his unattached drinking buddies

2 During the big game

3 Before his parents are coming over

4 When he's really sick

5 When he's dead

CHAPTER NINE

If Mama Ain't Happy, Ain't Nobody Happy!

Remember to be very careful of who you talk about around here. Everybody in the South is kin to each other. No matter who you bring up, you're bound to be insulting somebody's aunt, uncle, or third cousin twice removed.

—Anonymous

Unless you've been living under a rock somewhere, all of y'all have heard the jokes made about us down here in the South. They say we're just a bunch of inbreeds, and that we're all related to one another somehow. They say that we sleep with our uncles, and marry our cousins. I'm here to tell you that that is not entirely untrue, but for most of us, it's really not like that. (FYI, it happens mostly in Arkansas!) However, in the South, we cherish our family and our friends like no other people I know. So when it comes to huntin' down a man and holding on to him, you have to know how to win over his family and his buddies.

DADDY

All rightee, first you got the Daddy. Now remember, he's the head of the family, and he is in charge of what everybody else does. Actually, that's a big lie, because we all know that Mama is really in charge, but we just let Daddy think he is! But Daddy loves this illusion, so we don't do anything to burst his bubble. Daddy's biggest priorities are his wife and kids. He wants them safe, healthy, and happy. So when his boy meets a girl and wants to bring her home to meet the parents, Daddy just wants to make sure his "boy done good."

The Daddy is one of the easiest people in your man's close-knit group to impress and win over. First, you want to make sure that you have just enough sizzle that Daddy is thinking to himself, "Junior's got himself a great little number there," but you want him to think you're also sweet as sugar. He'll be watching to see how you treat his son. He'll want to know whether you're kind to him, if you laugh at his jokes and find him funny, and whether or not you let him be in charge. In other words, Daddy wants to make sure you're not going to be a pushy little bitch that's out to change him!

One way to win over Daddy is to ask about his "trophies." This can be anything from a wall in his house covered with pictures of the fish he caught in various bass-fishing tournaments to the mounted animals he has everywhere in the den. He may be a marathon runner, and have a showcase full of medals and ribbons. Whatever it is, get him to talk about it, and you'll have him eating out of the palm of your hand. I'm sure you've gotten this already, but let me remind you one more time: men are simple creatures, and there's nothing they like better than when you are stroking their egos. By the way, if you don't know anything about his hobby, it's perfectly okay to say so and let him teach you all about it. You'll get lots of points for that!

Oh yeah, here's a word of advice if Daddy is doing the cooking when you go over for dinner. While you will want to compliment him on his BBQ ribs, for example, resist the urge to give him any hints about how to make the sauce sweeter, or to make a suggestion about how the grilling should be done. The problem with this is that he may tell you to "go ahead and make a stab at it." If you oblige him, you're running the risk of doing two things: First, you may not be able to do it better than Daddy. Second, if Daddy absolutely loves what you've done, and thinks they are the best ribs he's ever had, you just might be slapping Mama in the face because the sauce was *her* original recipe. We'll talk more later about Mama and cooking, but I wanted to make sure you've been warned.

One more thing you ought to remember: When you're in the presence of Daddy, try not to crawl all over your man like white on rice. When in doubt, reduce your public displays of affection to a minimum, and keep your hands to yourself. Besides, Daddy's not stupid. He knows his boy has been around the block a time or two. But you don't want him thinking about how many times you've been around the block—or how many guys you've been around it with!

SIBLINGS

Sometimes when you go to meet his parents for the first time, his siblings will be there, too. First rule of thumb: make sure you haven't dated and/or slept with any of them. After all, depending on where you live, the world can be a mighty small place.

Second, follow your man's lead. If he is able to laugh and joke with his brother, you should be able to as well. If his sister is sensitive about certain topics, and you've observed your man keeping quiet, you should shut up, too. Basically, if you treat his family the way that he treats his family, you should be in good shape. The only time this rule doesn't apply is if he is having an argument with a brother or sister, and they aren't on good terms. Don't get caught up in his family drama, because we all know that these things don't last. Before you know it, they'll be best pals in the again in the blink of an eye, and you'll forever be labeled as the woman who criticized his family. I know it doesn't sound right or fair, but that's how it is. Family can criticize one another, but you can't, at least not in the beginning. Remember: Blood is thicker than water.

MAMA

Now, about Mama. This is the toughest nut you'll have to crack! You *cannot* outdo her, no matter how much she acts like she doesn't care if you do. She will *always* care, so do not fall for that trick! Remember, Mama was once in your shoes, so she knows how to throw out the bait and set the hook. And one day, you'll be doing the same to *your* son's best girl.

The key to charming Mama is that she needs to feel as if she's responsible for how your man turned out. After all, he sprang from her loins, and his very existence is a reflection on her. She wants you to know how perfect he is, and you need to be able to communicate back to her that of course, she's perfectly right. Pick out one thing that you know is important to Mama. Manners are usually a safe bet. All mamas want to believe that their son knows how to treat a lady!

One way to win over Mama is to compliment her style. It doesn't matter if she is a plain Jane or a real classy broad, you need to find a way to communicate that what she is wearing "looks perfect on her." If you feel that this defies your honest nature, then find another way to compliment her that doesn't offend you as much. For instance, you might say that the color red looks stunning on her and that you wish you could wear that color, but it simply looks awful on you. If you meet her in her home, you might compliment her decorating abilities. Again, you may not like it that she has plastic covering her couch, and that it burned your legs when you sat down and squeaked when you tried to shift. But there has got to be one complimentary thing that you can pick out, and when you find it, speak up.

Although it sounds silly and unreasonable, do *not* ask for any of her recipes unless she offers it to you first; otherwise, she may feel as if you're trying to take her place and outdo her. Instead, tell her that her potato salad is the best you've ever eaten, and how much her son has bragged about it.

Basically, it boils down to this: Mama is the one who is really in charge of the family, and everybody knows it. If Mama ain't happy, ain't nobody happy. That's the truth. She is the queen of her world, and any female that her son brings home is going to be seen as a bit of a threat to her. The trick is to be pleasant, likable, and flattering without usurping her place on the throne! You need to be the "Princess" to the "Queen" who is awaiting her son to become "King." Mind you, you're not really concerned about being the Queen as you are in supporting *her* son in being a good King!

So how can you gauge how you're doing with Mama? Well, every family is different. You might not know anything until afterward, when she gives your man a full report. But a surefire sign you're doing well with Mama is by how much information she shares with you about her son's history. If she starts telling stories or bringing out the picture albums, you have been accepted. If she shows you the baby pictures of Junior in the bathtub in his "full glory," there are two things you must remember. First, don't act like you see "it" all the time. Second, take this as a sign that Mama doesn't mind that you are seeing it now!

When my friend Amy met her boyfriend Dewey Wayne's mother, Ruby (named for her bright red hair), for the first time, she was very nervous. But she smiled prettily and told Ruby that she was glad to finally meet the woman that Dewey Wayne was always talking about.

When Dewy Wayne grabbed Ruby and hugged so tight that he pulled her right off the ground, Ruby threw Amy a look as if to say, "He'll always love me best." This made Amy even more nervous, but she put on her best smile and obliged when Ruby invited her to help set the table.

As Amy arranged the silverware, Ruby felt the need to remind her that the knives go on the right of the plates. Of course, Amy already knew this because of the etiquette classes her own mama had her take, but instead of saying so, she politely and cheerfully said, "Yes, ma'am!" So far so good.

When they sat down to dinner, Dewey Wayne gave Amy a little peck on her cheek. She smiled demurely, but pushed Dewey Wayne's hand away when he tried to pat her butt. "Stop that, mister!" she said, and playfully slapped his arm. Amy then mentioned to Ruby that the linen blouse she was wearing was "so cute and colorful." Ruby smiled widely and thanked her. She mentioned that she got it at her favorite store, and then if Amy liked, she could call to see if they had any more of them in stock.

This, dear readers, is where Amy almost dropped the ball. Before she could stop herself, she responded, "Oh, I'd *never* wear that!" Ruby tensed and her upper lip twitched. There were a couple of seconds of horrid silence, but Amy, being pretty quick on her feet, recovered and said, "There's no way somebody my size could pull that off." You could see Ruby's shoulders visibly relax and the smile returned to her face. She responded, "Nonsense, but thank you, dear." A great recovery for Amy!

As the baked beans were being passed around, Amy gushed about how wonderful they smelled. She had two helpings even though she was full as a tick. Amy even said that there had to be secret ingredients to Ruby's recipe, because Amy never could get her beans so full of flavor. As she was helping Ruby with the dishes in the kitchen after dinner, Ruby told Amy that she was a bright girl. Amy thanked her and asked her why she thought that. Ruby indicated that she did indeed have a secret ingredient for her baked beans, and that the next time she came over, she'd write it down for Amy. Translation: "I like you, but I don't like you enough—yet."

Now, all in all, Amy did a good job winning over Dewey's mama. But here are a couple of other examples about how *not* to win over Mama:

Never upstage a mama in her own kitchen. Sara Beth had loved chess pie ever since she was knee-high to a grasshopper. Her grandmother's recipe made the sugary mixture melt effortlessly in your mouth, and Sara Beth couldn't get enough of it. So when her new boyfriend Jack invited her for dinner with his parents, she decided she'd take a dessert. Surely she thought this would be seen as a lovely gesture, and Sara Beth would be seen as a thoughtful young lady.

Well, as you might imagine, this is not how it turned out. When Jack's mama, Laura, saw Sara Beth's chess pie, she gave her most gracious smile and said, "What a surprise. Did Jack tell you to bring this?" Sara Beth said that it was her grandmother's recipe and the most incredible pie she'd ever eaten.

Sara Beth was feeling pretty good about things until she walked into the kitchen and saw another chess pie sitting on the counter. It turns out that Jack's mama makes a killer chess pie as well, and Jack had forgotten to mention this to Sara Beth. Again, Mama remained calm about it and said for Sara Beth not to worry about it. She would simply serve both pies for dessert.

The contest was on. As pieces of the pie were served all around, Sara Beth held her breath. After a few minutes, it became clear that Sara Beth's pie was the favorite because Jack and his daddy had her pie plus second helpings, but Mama was none too happy, judging by the accusatory stare she had planted on her husband.

Sara Beth had to think fast. In her quest to remedy the situation, she made Jack eat three pieces of his mama's pie and she had two pieces herself. She was sick all afternoon but at least Mama's pie got eaten and the relationship between Sara Beth and Jack was saved!

Then there was my pal, Sally. Bless her heart, she doesn't have the sense God gave a billy goat. When Howard invited her over for Sunday lunch after church, he mentioned that his mama made the best mashed potatoes this side of the Mississippi. Sally countered that he hadn't had *her* potatoes. In an effort to impress Howard, she make a big ol' pot of mashed potatoes and proudly presented them to Howard's mama when she entered her home, saying, "I can't wait for you to try these!" You should have seen Mama's face when it became red as a beet. She clenched her teeth, thanked Sally, and took the potatoes to the kitchen. Interestingly, she managed to "forget" to bring them to the table until her own potatoes had been passed around. When Sally realized they were missing, she still didn't get the message, so she went and got them. Not a soul took a helping because they were all smart enough not to cross Mama and her prize-winning taters!

Keep it covered! Remember how I told you that upon meeting a man's parents, it's okay to dress attractively, but you don't want to show off all you've got? Well, Esther had a mishap with a

bathing suit when she went to Tom's family's Fourth of July celebration at their lake house. All of his brothers and sisters, eight of
them, were going to be there. Esther was very well endowed.
Now, every girl I know was jealous of Esther and how she could
fill out a bikini. But knowing that this might not be appropriate
for the first meeting with Tom's parents, she bought a conservative, one-piece black bathing suit.

But in her excitement over meeting Tom's family, she absent-
mindedly packed the wrong bathing suit. Tom's family's house
was in the middle of nowhere, and there wasn't a store for miles
around. So, against her better judgment, Esther went ahead and put
on her itsy-bitsy bikini and went out to join the family on the dock.

Now, since Tom has five brothers, there were more tongues
hanging out than a bunch of bluetick hounds at a meat market!
Tom's father was none too subtle, either. Well, you know what
that means. Mama and the other females in the group were so
jealous and pissed off that they could barely see straight. Tom's
mama couldn't take it anymore. She gave Esther a big, green, ugly
T-shirt, saying she might want to put it on to prevent getting sun-
burned. As their relationship progressed, Esther remembered not
to upstage these gals, and things moved along smoothly.

Don't share cute stories about you and your man. No mama
wants to hear that her son is a good kisser or how he romanced his
gal right out of her clothes! Keep these details to yourself, or if you
are about to burst with excitement because you just have to tell
somebody, tell your girlfriends!

Lynn had been dating Chuck for about three months. They were quite a passionate pair and, among their friends, they were already becoming famous for displaying a lot of PDA—public displays of affection. When Chuck said he'd like Lynn to meet his mom, the three agreed to have lunch at the club. The meeting started out all right. Lynn watched to see if Mama ordered a cocktail at lunch, and when she did, Lynn followed suit. Everything was going along swimmingly, and Lynn was pretty sure that Chuck's mama liked her. Chuck excused himself to go have a smoke at the bar.

When he left, Chuck's mama mentioned that her son seemed to be enamored of Lynn. She further said that they complemented each other well. Lynn, tipsy from one too many Bloody Marys, giggled, and placed her hand on Mama's arm. She said in a conspiratorial whisper, "Why, he is the most romantic man I know. He makes everything exciting. Why, I shouldn't say anything (she should've stopped right there!), but Chuck took me parking behind the Methodist church the other night because he simply couldn't wait 'til we got home. Wouldn't you just know it? The minister knocked on the window and had to ask us to leave. Isn't that the funniest thing?"

I guess I don't have to tell you that it *wasn't* at all the funniest thing. Mama looked as if she were about to throw up right then and there. When Chuck joined them at the table, Mama was fanning herself and chirped, "Well, son, I hear that Reverend Jackson got to meet your fine young lady." Needless to say, the luncheon ended on a tense note!

Here's How You Do It Right

Blythe was invited to meet Jim's parents over a weekend trip to his home. She had the good sense to pay attention to what she was packing, so the bathing suit problem was never an issue. But she did know that Jim's mother loved to sew. Jim told her that she had made all the curtains in the family's home and that people always thought they were made by a professional. Blythe made sure that a pair of pants that she took with her had a hem that was partially out. As they all retired to their bedrooms to get dressed for dinner that night at the local restaurant, Blythe asked Jim's mama if she would show her how to hem her pants because she couldn't wear them the way they were. Jim's mama had no intention of making Blythe hem her own pants and instead offered to do them for her. Blythe gently resisted, but Mama insisted, and so they sat together while she repaired the pants.

Then there is my friend Lisa. She had met Allen's mother and father a couple of months ago and their initial encounter was by all accounts, on both sides, very pleasant and successful. Allen is an only child, and has been quite close to his parents all of his life. Allen's mother mentioned at least twice that she hardly ever saw Allen anymore, what with his busy career and new girlfriend and all. Lisa also learned that Allen's mama loves the opera. However, she didn't go very often because Allen's father would rather poke himself in the eye with a stick than sit through "such a tortuous experience."

Well, Lisa was on her toes during that conversation and stored that tidbit of information in the back of her brain. She then encouraged Allen to begin taking his mother to lunch regularly, just the two of them. Allen said that he had never thought of doing that, and it would be a great way to spend some time with his mother. Then Lisa won the lottery of all lotteries when she planned this next one out. She found out that a popular opera was coming to town and some famous opera singer was starring in it. She bought two tickets for Allen and his mother. Allen was, it suffices to say, frustrated because he didn't like the opera, either. He suggested that Lisa should go and take his mother. Lisa refused, saying that this is something his mother enjoys and that Alan should "do this one thing."

Before Allen and his mother left for the opera, Lisa told Allen not to tell his mother that she had made these suggestions and these arrangements. Allen understood that she was trying to let him take the credit and he gratefully agreed. Their opera date was a smashing success. A few weeks later, after several lunches with his mother, Allen confessed that it was Lisa's idea for him to see her more often. He even told her that Lisa had bought the tickets for the opera. Needless to say, Lisa was definitely in!

FRIENDS

Well, we got the family out of the way, but you still have to meet your man's other family—his friends, the "buds," his partners in crime, the "gang." In this group are several categories of friends that you need to be ready to deal with if you want to win your man over, including the drinkin' buddies, the work buddies, the best friend, the best gal-pal, and the dog (not necessarily in order of importance!), and more.

Drinking Buddies

These are the guys with whom your man makes an obnoxious ass out of himself every time he is with them. Whether they're watching football, fishing, or just sitting around the house, they do just about everything together as long as alcohol is involved. Some may already be married, others may have girlfriends, and there will be a stray or two who are just dating around. When your man starts to date, he inevitably will be a lot less available to them, which means they may get jealous of the time that your man is spending with you. There is also the fear that their buddy will become "whipped," as they say, and won't be allowed to be a member of the drinking gang anymore.

So how do you convince these guys that you're not a threat, and that you don't mind if your man spends time with them? Oh, in case I forgot to explain, you *cannot* ask your man to quit seeing them. These are his buddies, and while they may be a gross bunch of idiots, you have no right to ask him to give up his friends. If you want to bring them into the fold, you have to convince them that you don't perceive them as a threat.

So how do you do it? Make them *feel* like he is still part of them even though he is taking time away from them to be with you. If you know that all of your boyfriend's buddies like basketball, you might get them tickets to a basketball game. Or you might offer to cook dinner for them before sending them off to the game. If you know that they are going to a particular bar, call the bartender and ask to have the first round of drinks put on your credit card for them. In other words, do something for all of them that includes your boyfriend and does *not* include you. Incidentally, if you bought them tickets to some sort of outing and they invite you because they're trying to be nice, simply say no. They don't really want you there, but there is a sense of guilt that they feel because *now* they're taking your boyfriend away from you.

Oh, and before I forget, my friend Steve wants me to pass on this piece of advice to all of you: Don't try to fix up your boyfriend's buddies. You see, when Steve was dating Kerri, he got himself into a situation because she mentioned that she wanted her friend Roxanne, to go out with his friend Brad. She was convinced that they'd make the "perfect couple." Against his better judgment, Steve agreed. The evening was a mess. Roxanne revealed that she hadn't had a date in three years, became sloppy drunk, and started to talk about all the bad men "out there." Then she made a move on Brad, who was too stunned to move. It was real ugly! Like Steve says, you simply cannot make your man's buddies as happy as your man—you'll only be asking for trouble!

It's also good to remember that the way your boyfriend treats you when the two of you are alone is likely to be vastly different than when he's with his drinkin' buddies. They do not usually bring out the best in one another, and generally encourage each other to act as juvenile as possible.

Work Buddies

If your man wants to take you to a business function, take his lead. If he works with a conservative group of uptight professionals, this is not the time to wear your new silk lingerie-look-alike cocktail dress that is cut up to "there." At any type of work function, you're better off wearing something that doesn't make you stand out, and certainly that will not detract from your boyfriend's presence. The best rule of thumb is to know a little bit about what the rest of your boyfriend's colleagues do, so that you can ask some intelligent questions. If he works at the Home Depot, know your tools. If he's a lawyer, understand a little legal jargon like what kind of law the firm handles—corporate, family, etc. And, important here, don't overdo the booze. A drunk, slurring, drooling girlfriend is not likely to help her boyfriend score any points with his boss. You'll be fine as long as you stay "below the radar."

Make sure that if you are drinking with the work buddies that you don't make an ass of yourself. This is not the time to match them drink for drink even though you're pretty sure you could win the game! You don't have to make a scene, showing your disgust of their behavior. If you are worried that your man is getting in too deep, gently suggest to him that you can't wait to get him alone. That usually does the trick, and he will be ready to go. If it doesn't work, it's okay to excuse yourself and get a cab, but not before you bid everyone good night!

Gal Pals

A guy's best gal-pal is fiercely protective of her male friend. The most that you can hope for is that she does not chew you up and spit you out without giving you an opportunity to prove yourself worthy of being this man's girlfriend.

This is not the time to show jealousy or to feel intimidated by having another female around. If you're a jealous type of girl, you're going to have a hard time. Be as honest and direct as she is going to be with you, and even if the two of you really hit it off, remember that she'll always be his friend first, so proceed with caution! Never ask her any questions about your boyfriend's old girlfriends. It's never safe to go fishing in those waters! Don't try to suck up to her, because she will spot your superficial attempts from a mile away. All you can really do is pray and hope it just goes well. When she sees that your intentions are true and you are exactly how you seem, she will start cutting you some slack.

His Best Friend

What can you say about a best friend? This is the person who brings out the best in you, and is the person you can count on through thick and thin. Even though men may not have as much emotional depth as we girls do, they still have best friends. They are different from the gal-pal, though, because gal-pals often mother their male friends. And just like Mama, they aren't sure anyone will be good enough. If you want to be liked by your man's best friend, just like it is with the gal-pal, now is not the time to turn it up a notch and pretend to be something you're not. Be yourself, draw him out by asking questions about him, about how the two of them met, or something else of interest to him. Your man's best friends will like you simply because he likes you. He won't judge you or worry that he needs to protect his friend. As long as you are good to his friend and as long as you show yourself to be true blue, the best friend will turn out to be your biggest ally.

Canine Companions

Ah, there's something about a man and his dog! A man has undying devotion for his dog. So how do you win over the dog? Actually, it's quite simple. First of all, let's hope you like dogs because they can smell it on you if you don't. Dogs love attention, so the best trick is to love on the dog before you love on your man. Bring treats with you when you see him. Play his favorite game of catch or tug if that's what he enjoys. Keep his "baby" when your man is out of town. Take him to his favorite park, and offer to give Fido a bath. A man will turn to jelly when he thinks someone else believes his dog is as perfect as he does.

There's really no way to separate a man from his family or friends when he truly cares about them. Like I said earlier, you shouldn't even try. If you want to win over your man, you'll do well to remember he is a package deal. You'll have to take the whole package, or none at all.

Top 5 Things a Man's Family Doesn't Need to Know

1 You met in a bar

2 Your father, mother, brother, or sister have been in prison

3 You have been to rehab

4 That there ever was another man in your life

5 Your bra size

CHAPTER TEN

"Pull My Finger": *Communicating* *with Your Man*

Lettin' the cat outta the bag is a whole lot easier than puttin' it back in.

—Southern saying

There's an old story that goes something like this. A woman had to tell her husband the same piece of information three times within a five-minute period. When it became obvious to her that he still wasn't listening, she became frustrated and admonished him. "You never hear a word I say." He looked up from what he was doing and responded, "Huh?"

Yep, that's how communicating with a man can be. A man can drive you to the very edge of insanity with what can only appear to be his incapability or his refusal to engage in verbal conversation. Talking to a man is like talking to a turtle. You're sure there's something under that shell, but you're just not convinced you're getting through. It's just damn exasperating! And it's universal—men everywhere are like this!

I did some research because I wanted to know how many words a man speaks versus how many words a woman speaks in a day. So I went to my most trusted source, *Cosmopolitan* magazine. Okay, I could've gone to more intellectual spots, but who can resist the pages of *Cosmo* and its wise words for women! In 2004, the editor in chief of *Cosmo* estimated that men speak between 2,000 and 4,000 words a day, whereas women speak 6,000 to 8,000 words a day. I don't know about you, but this tells me two things:

1. Women are obviously smarter and have the ability to use more words in the English language.

2. Men just don't say much.

A woman can take the English language and make it her own so that she has a unique way of talking and getting her messages across. Men use as few words as possible, as if it saps all of their energy to come up with them. A woman feels the need to share just about everything that's going on in her life. For example, a female may say, "I have cut my hand and it's gushing blood, and I need to go to the ER now, for stitches!" From that statement, we know exactly what she means and there is no room for misinterpretation. When a man says, "It's just a small cut," it could mean that he really did suffer a small cut. Or it could mean that he needs stitches. A man will wait until he needs stitches or major surgery to communicate a problem. Only when it is truly important does he say anything. There is one exception to this rule, however, and that's when he's really, really sick, which for a man means having a cold. Then he will whine in his most pathetic voice, "I feel awful." Then he'll drag himself to bed and expects you to wait on him hand and foot. It should be noted that when he has acute appendicitis, a man is rarely too sick for sex and *will* expect that to be part of your nursing duties, if your relationship has reached that point. If you're inclined to catch what he's got, go ahead. Otherwise, parrot what your mama told you when you were a child. "If you're too sick to go to school, you're not going to play, either!"

When a man starts talking too much, you can bet he's hiding something. This does not mean that he's lying about something, but for sure he does not want to discuss whatever it is that's going on. Go ahead, check it out if you don't believe me, but I think you will find that I'm right! Darlin', if he's carrying on a conversation about your clothes, your girlfriends, your family, or how the house is decorated—well, girl, you'd better start digging, because there's something he's trying to cover up, like a dog with a ham bone!

Another simple truth about men and communication is that men want to fix things. They want to fix tires that are flat, replace windows that are broken, and mend the wobbly legs on the kitchen table. That's pretty easy to understand, right? Well, when it comes to communication, they're the same way.

Let me give you some examples:

She says: "I hate my job and those people. Nothing I do seems right so I don't know why I bother!"
He says: "Well, you could always quit."
She says: "I feel so fat, so bloated, so ugly. I just want to hide."
He says: "Why don't you buy some new clothes in a bigger size?" (You only need to be a woman to understand how he just screwed up—big time!)

She says: "Have you seen all the junk the neighbors have in their front yard? I have half a mind to set it all on fire. Plus the whole damn mess makes our house look like we're messy, too!"

He says: "Well, then, let's move." (Is he crazy? Once again, she's just upset—give us a break, guys!)

The difference is that a man thinks there needs to be the perfect solution to all problems. And if he can come up with one that is over-the-top, he feels as if he has rescued and saved his beloved. Women just want to talk it out—that's what we do. And we're willing to talk as long as it takes. For a man, five minutes is probably the maximum time he'll give a conversation before it's over for him. (Now, ladies, let's try not to draw any analogy between a man's conversational skills and his sexual performance here!)

In order to communicate effectively with your man, you need to know the five statements that every man uses at least once in his lifetime, but really, probably more than that. Since their communication skills are limited, the few words they do manage to speak need to be understood by you so that you can respond appropriately.

1.   **"Wanna see the shelves I built?"** Ladies, this is the typical "I need attention and want you to shower me with compliments about what I've done" comment. A man simply must have his ego stroked, and, if you're his woman, he expects *you* to do the stroking. It can be something as simple as hanging a painting or cleaning up the kitchen for you, but he needs you to notice. Let's

be honest, we girls can be shameless about begging for attention ourselves, so we really can't blame a guy for wanting the same thing. When your man walks up to you and asks you to look at what he's done, he's just about as puffed up with pride as the little boy who just discovered he has a penis! Is it really going to hurt you that much to praise him? After all, it doesn't cost anything, it doesn't take a lot of time, and it makes him think you really "get" him.

2. **"Can we talk about this later?"** Believe it or not, when a man asks this question, he really means it! We women cannot let anything go. If we want to talk about something, we've got to exhaust it thoroughly before we are ready to stop. When a man remarks that we should discuss something later, most of us take that as a challenge. We stay after him, follow him out of the room, and even yell our comments if necessary. You might as well save your breath, though, because he has already tuned you out. Plus, he's hoping that if you agree to talk about it later, there's a chance you might forget what you wanted to say altogether. He should be so lucky!

My friend Lucy once barricaded her husband in the bedroom after he uttered those alarming words. She told him that he wasn't going anywhere until she was finished telling what she had to say. You would have thought he would have been a captive audience, but not so. He sat down calmly on the bed, and from the corner of his eye, he spied a *Better Homes and Gardens* on the bedside table. While Lucy was ranting and raving and even shedding some tears, he nonchalantly picked up the magazine and began to peruse it. It wasn't until Lucy grabbed it from his hands and hit him over the head with it that he realized it was time to listen.

My best advice when a man utters this phrase is to take it literally, and then do the unthinkable—keep your mouth shut. I know what you want to talk about is probably earth shattering, but you're really not going to get through to him when he's in this mind-set.

3. **"You must have PMS."** We've all heard it. The words may change, and yet it all means the same thing, and is just as offensive no matter how it is said. These are the dreaded words that none of us wants to hear, but they inevitably come out of every man's mouth sooner or later. Other variations include, "Is it that time of the month for you?" Or "Is your period on its way?" Or "Is your Aunt Flo visiting?"

What's funny to me is that a man can ask this question at least once a week, which tells me he doesn't even know how to do the math! The minute that we say something that he doesn't like, or we sound remotely bitchy, he immediately wants to blame it on our being female.

You have to admit, however, that during that time of the month, we are not at our most likable. Let's face it. We are swollen up like an overfed slug, our breath stinks, the tiniest irritant is magnified ten thousand times, and we cry at the drop of a hat. Personally, I think that during this time we deserve to be pampered rather than accosted. Men are dumber than a turnip seed, and ought to be damn glad they don't have to suffer from this af-fliction! As mad as it makes you, don't take it too personally. It's probably the best thing they can come up with at the time. Kinda makes you feel sorry for them when you think about it that way, doesn't it? Think about it: you can search far and wide, but you'll never find a man who could put up with our "monthlies" as hero-ically as we do! So when your man says this, resist the urge to grab him where it really hurts. Smile sweetly, even if it's through clenched teeth, and respond calmly. Not only will this throw him off be-cause he expects you to blow him to kingdom come, but you also will have caused him to lose his excuse to blame you for something *he's* really done!

4. "Honey, I'm in the middle of something." It doesn't mat-ter if you just spotted a rat, discovered your dog ate one of your de-signer shoes, or you had a fight with your best friend. He simply does not want to listen to you until he is finished with what he's doing, whether its reloading his shotgun, tying a fly to his fishing pole, or scratching his crotch. How many times do I have to tell you? Men are simple creatures, and multitasking is not one of their talents.

You wonder how men make it through this world doing only one thing at a time. A woman can shave her legs, apply makeup, and get dressed, all while having a phone conversation. In fact, we can carry on two conversations at the same time and not miss a beat. Not so with the male species. Unless you're on fire or you are about to die, I wouldn't even try to fight this one. Next time he gives you this line, do what I do, which I think is an entirely mature approach. Roll your eyes, stick your tongue out at him, and flip him the bird. Then hold your head up high, and walk away. That'll teach him!

5. **"That's not what I meant."** Ahh! Behold the most frequent, most pathetic, and most frequently used statement men make. Give me a break! If a man uses approximately one-fourth to one-third the amount of words we do each day, then obviously they mean what they are saying.

Personally, I find the perfect thing to do when he uses this statement is to say nothing. After all, silence is golden, and there's nothing quite like those humiliating, embarrassing few seconds of silence when it finally dawns on him that he made a rather large boo-boo. I like to raise one eyebrow, stare at him to communicate that saying, "That's not what I meant" was incredibly stupid, and then shake my head in disgust. Usually, if a man has half a brain, he'll realize that he is caught, and he will try to pull himself out of a hole. It's up to you to decide if you want to rescue him or not. I wouldn't if I were you, but then sometimes I just enjoy watching a man squirm!

So how do you communicate effectively with your man so he will listen and be able to hold his attention longer than the average insect? As it happens, we Southern belles, being conversational gurus and all, know five easy things that any woman can do to ensure success.

1. Keep it short. If a man asks what you did today, what he really wants to know are the highlights, and I mean *only* the highlights. If you went out to lunch with an old friend, you do not need to tell him what was on the menu, what you ordered, and how it gave you gas. You don't have to include every piece of conversation that you and your pal had, nor does he care that the restroom was smelly. He does not need the details and he certainly is not interested in them!

Talking to a man is like giving directions. A man wants you to tell him how to get from point A to point B, in the quickest, most efficient, and straightforward method possible. When a woman wants instructions, she wants to hear more. After all, she might want to meander along, stop at a little antique shop, and maybe even get a bite of lunch. Men don't care about any of that.

How do you know if you're saying too much? If you see that glazed, "Get me out of here" look on his face, you've lost him. Keep it short, and your man is more likely to hear you and be responsive.

2. Keep it simple. I know this may sound much like the "keeping it short rule," but it's different. Because a man can become quickly overwhelmed by too much information, you need to be able to communicate with recognizable, easy words, preferably ones that have as few syllables as possible! This is not the time to impress him with your expansive vocabulary, because it will go largely unappreciated. Consider the word "audacious." For a man, this may be a big word. If he appears to have no clue what you mean by that, don't use other words he won't understand to define that one. That means you should stay away from "doughty, valorous, and intrepid." Instead, just say, "bold." There's no reason to make your man feel stupid, and I know that word may not have the punch that "audacious" has, but you will be able to make your point anyway. Men just aren't impressed with that sort of thing. They are way more interested in how "comely" you are (for any man who might be reading this now, that means "beautiful").

3. **Pick your venue.** This means that you need to find the perfect place or the occasion in which your man will be the most receptive to what you are about to say. For example, if he's watching the football game with his buddies, this is not the time for you to tell him that he promised to go to the mall with you this weekend. Not only is it embarrassing, but he is likely to blow you off, thinking you are merely trying to be funny in front of his friends. Likewise, in the middle of sex, don't ask him if he'll help you rehearse a speech you've got to give the next morning at a big meeting. This is like a cold shower! Also, the mood will be gone, and he'll be offended that your brain is elsewhere. Don't give bad news or address a sticky issue as he's walking out the door, especially if he's late. He won't hear half of what you are saying, and you'll be forcing him to say the old, "Can we talk about this later?"

You may be saying to yourself, "Duh, she doesn't need to be telling me this." You're right, but I bet you *do* need a little reminding. When something is on our minds, we women like to say it as soon as it comes up. But it's not always the right time, and your choice of venue has a lot to do with whether or not you'll be heard, and whether the response will be what you want. Remember, men just aren't up to multitasking, so trying to talk to them at the wrong place and time is really putting them to the test. So if they fail that test, you really have no one to blame but yourself.

4. Keep your perspective. This is probably a lesson for life, but it certainly will help in your communications with your man. This means that you pick your battles. Is it more important to complain about his inability to pick up his dirty socks off the bedroom floor or remember that he thoughtfully filled your gas tank for you the night before? Okay, so sometimes he makes an ass out of himself in front of your friends. If you're the only one who's embarrassed, let it go. If you think you know more than he does about a particular issue, you don't always have to tell him. Wait until he asks, or refer to the rules above and plunge right in. The point is that not everything has to be discussed right now, or ever.

Part of keeping your perspective is maintaining your sense of humor. This will serve you well when you find yourself mystified by some of the things he says and does. Ask yourself if the battle or issue you're about to bring up will really matter in a year. If the answer is no, then back off. Your man already has a mother—he really doesn't need another.

5. Take one for the team. Southern belles are not fragile little flowers that wilt at the first sign of trouble and say, "I'm sorry," just to smooth things over! Taking one for the team means doing what is best for you and your man. So, if saying a simple "It was my fault," or "I'm sorry" is helpful, do it. I'm not saying you have to be insincere about it, but come on. Is every fight or issue between you so important that you can't let it go? Is your pride bigger than your desire for a happy relationship? If you can't bear to say you're sorry for something you know you didn't do, and it goes against your moral compass to do it, how about trying, "You might be right." God knows, it may hurt like hell coming out of your mouth, but it can go a long way toward mending fences with your man. There's also that extra benefit of letting him keep on believing he was right and you were wrong. Even though we know the truth, no one has to be the wiser!

Oh, and by the way, when the tables are turned and he "takes one for the team," try to be gracious about it. If he says he's sorry, accept it and move on. Don't gloat and don't dwell on it. Don't go on and on about the other things he *should* be sorry for—you do not have to give him a checklist to make sure he's made proper amends.

So there you are, ladies. Communication 101 with a man, Southern belle style. If you follow my advice, he'll be hanging on your every word!

Top 5 Situations Where a Southern Belle Can Expect to Hear "Damn, Baby, That Was Great!"

1 After dinner

2 After a sports event

3 After an action movie

4 After a phenomenal bowel movement (really)

5 After sex

CHAPTER ELEVEN

Setting the Hook:
Last Lessons

The hardest task of a girl's life, nowadays, is to prove to a man that his intentions are serious.

—Helen Rowland

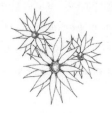

Now that I've taught you my best tricks and, hopefully, now that you have worked diligently to become more bellelike, it's time for you to decide if you *really* want to keep him for the long haul. Down here, every Southern woman has at least been hunting or has been around hunters. There are three kinds of hunters—which one are you? Quail Hunter? Duck Hunter? Deer Hunter? One is not any better than the other, but each has different ways to bag her prey!

QUAIL HUNTER

Here's the thing about a quail hunter—they're out in the field, on the move, and looking for the game to flush. He may take his favorite dog with him to locate the coveys, but everyone knows he'll be the one to make the kill. There's not much stealth or skill involved here—it's all about getting the job done.

If you're a Quail Hunter, you are the kind of woman who comes on strong and isn't afraid to pull out all the stops. You are the kind who is willing to make it clear up front that you expect a future with him. You are not hesitant to ask questions—the whens, wheres, and hows. Your words and your behavior leave a man with absolutely no doubts as to where you hope the two of you are headed.

So when you're out with your best friend, and on a manhunt, you're dressed for the kill and are out there beating the bushes for the birds (men) to flush. Usually when the quail flush, they make a lot of noise and try to fly away—sort of like a man that thinks he wants to stay a bachelor. Your job is to bring him down and put him in the game bag. Quail hunting is tough and takes a lot of walking and beating the bushes. But what a tasty treat when you get him in the pan!

My friend Nancy is the perfect example of a Quail Hunter. She's a direct and all-business kind of woman. She sets goals, even in her romantic endeavors, and works hard to achieve them. Before she met John, Nancy had been through nine serious relationships that she thought were permanent. But it turned out, the men couldn't deal with Nancy's strength. John, or Number 10 as we like to call him, came along, and we were certain he wouldn't survive her no-nonsense approach to romance. But time after time, he matched her one for one with his very own single-minded stance about how romances should evolve. Luckily for both of them, they were on the same path and it finally worked.

I must warn you, though. For the most part, men are intensely terrified by this kind of a woman. In order to keep them comfortable, soften your assertiveness so that you do not sound harsh and unyielding. Find a way to say things assertively that won't put others on the defensive, and make your man feel it's a challenge to hunt after you. Unless your man is independent, open minded, and sees a woman as his complete equal, leave this kind of huntin' to someone else.

THE DUCK HUNTER

Now, unlike flushing out quail, duck hunting involves a lot of trickery and concealment. If you're a Duck Hunter, you're all camouflaged up and hiding in a well-concealed blind. You've got your decoys out and you're just waiting for the game to come into what they think is a really attractive place. So you want to be the place where the men (ducks) want to come to and you want to make that place damned intriguing. As he gets interested, he starts circling for a landing. Then BAM! There you are, standing up fully armed (or in this case, in a somewhat revealing outfit). He has no idea you are there—he doesn't even know you are hunting when you bag him.

Suzy was a great Duck Hunter before she bagged Hunter (that really is his name, even though he was the game, in this case!). Hunter and Suzy had been around each other for months in a mutual friendship kind of group. Soon, Suzy found herself fancying Hunter and decided she wanted to pursue him. So one night, Suzy put on the dog (that means she dressed up really nice) and showed up at the bar just late enough that she was the main focus when she joined the group. Her decoys (her three best friends, in this case) had arranged the seating so that when she arrived, her only available seat was directly across from Hunter. Suzy has fantastic cleavage and knew how to display it. Hunter fell right into the decoy spread, couldn't keep his eyes off of Suzy, and was a "dead duck" before the night was through!

If you are a Duck Hunter, like Suzy, you have your tricks to get the duck to come to you. Ducks are smart. You have to set out decoys to attract them, and then you must sit and wait for them! In human terms, you have to set out decoys, too.

Once you decide he is *the* one, one decoy you can use is your time. Offer more of it to him to attend to his needs. I'm not saying you have to give up your life, and I'd have to kill you if you did! What you want to accomplish is making your man happy so that he'll be glad that you're the only woman in his life. He will wonder how he ever got along without you!

Another decoy is your attention. Letting him know that he is the only thing on your mind at present is a powerful tool. Who doesn't like to be the most special person in another's world?

Another decoy might be sex, but I have generally found that this should be a last resort. Unless you plan on continuing to be the same sex kitten you are while catching your man, this could lead to disappointment for both of you.

If you're a Duck Hunter, it's okay to have some expectations. You will need to see if there is a natural progression occurring that makes you want a future with this guy. Is it okay to ask, "Where is this going?" Absolutely, but don't be obvious. This is a good and valid question, but use your head. Your man will soon know what you want, and he can give you an answer. If this relationship is not going anywhere, then you can move to another duck blind.

THE DEER HUNTER

The deer hunter is patient and selective. Part of any deer hunter's job is to sit very still and wait for the right one to come by. Concealment is important, but being in the right spot for the right buck is simply a matter of good planning. But you have to wear bright orange (deer are colorblind) and keep an eye out for the other hunters—because deer hunters use high-powered rifles—and you don't want to be in another hunter's territory. A really good deer hunter might let four or five really nice bucks go by, waiting for the right one. So if you're the Deer Hunter type of gal, you are not afraid to be in a predominantly male environment—and you're not afraid of a little healthy competition during the hunt!

For example, when Alice bagged Bucky (okay, his name was not Bucky, it was Theodore—but "Bucky" makes a much better name for this story!), Alice had decided to go hunting at a NASCAR race. Now there were plenty of other "hunters" out there (and Alice tells me they were Daisy Mae dressed—everything too short and too tight), but they respected each other's territories. Let's just say that when sweet-smelling, soft-skinned Alice set her sights on Bucky who was standing at a track railing, and sidled up to him, he was dead meat and ready to be mounted on the wall!

Are you a Deer Hunter? If you are, then you will want to attend to his needs, but after a time, you must back off a bit and sit very still. Let him take care of himself. For example, if you've been doing all of his laundry, let him try it on his own. Give him the opportunity and time to appreciate you. Be patient. Then he will realize that not only do you make his life complete, he will also feel that you are giving him space and time to miss you. I promise you he'll want you more as a result.

No matter what you do, whether you want to marry your man or not, remember this. Let your man have a life independent of yours. Love him and let him breathe. You don't want a man to feel as if you can't live a minute without him or if you're attached to his hip. Second, don't think you can change him, at least not most of him! If you want him, take him as you find him. Otherwise, let someone else have him.

There's a saying that goes like this—character is how we act when no one is watching. Before you determine that *this* is the man you want, observe him carefully. Is he kind to others? Does he respect his family? Does he respect you? Does he think you hung the moon? If you can answer these questions truthfully, then hold tightly onto him.

Well, I guess that about wraps it up. Southern belles certainly know how to get their man and their charms are known the world over. Now *you* can learn them, too. So hold your head up high, get yourself together, and get out there! Good luck! I can't wait to hear how it turns out for you.

Top 5 Reasons a Southern Belle Should Let Go of Her "Prey"

1   His kisses don't sizzle

2   He gets drunk on nearly every date

3   You've never met his parents

4   He's married

5   He criticizes your clothes, makeup, hair—we only let family go there!

Your guide to understanding the Southern lingo in this book!

3 pickles shy of a quart—His elevator doesn't go all the way to the top. He's so dumb he ain't got the sense God gave a billy goat. In other words, he's *dumb!*

A litter—A bunch of kids.

Big as all daylights—Humongous.

Bless your heart!—Come on, do you really need help with this one?

Blush like a Georgia peach—When peaches from Georgia are in season, they have the most gentle and beautiful color. When a Southern belle blushes, this is how she is said to look.

Country as a turnip green—A person who is country through and through.

Dang-it—Damn it to hell!

Dogs are barkin'—My feet are hurtin'!

Don't go fishin' where fish ain't biting—Don't bother looking for something in a place where you are not going to find it.

Don't go off with your pistol half-cocked—Don't do something without thinking it through.

Duck fit—Conniption fit; a really big tantrum

Dumber than a bucket of rocks—Can't get much dumber than this!

Dumber than a turnip seed—*Dumber* than a bucket of rocks. You get my point, right? Unless *you* are dumber than . . . oh well, never mind. *See also* Thick as bricks.

Dumb up—To act stupid or pretend to be dumb.

Drunker than a skunk—Well, I can't say I've ever seen a drunk skunk, but you get the picture!

Drunker than Cooter Brown—You don't need to know anything else about Cooter Brown. You just need to know he was drunker than hell!

Fixin'—About to do something.

Full as a tick—have you ever seen a tick? Those little varmints are teeny tiny! When you are full as a tick, you're gonna explode!

Gumption—Nerve, or balls, if you'll pardon my language!

Hell-bent—Gonna do it no matter what anybody says.

Hell's half-acre—I'm assuming hell is a big place, so half an acre there probably goes on forever!

Highfalutin—Someone who is too big for their britches; thinks they're something else!

Higher the hair, closer to God—You're read about the big hair—need I say more?

Hold your head up high even if your pockets are empty—In other words, just 'cause you haven't got anything doesn't mean you shouldn't be proud.

Knee-high to a grasshopper—A very young child.

Knickers in a knot—*See also* Panties in a bunch.

Lay up with—Have sex with.

Like a beagle after a rabbit—Wanting it real bad.

Lower than a snake's belly—You can't get much lower to the ground than a snake's belly! When you *do* get this low, you are a pretty despicable creature!

More important than lemonade and sunshine—Meaning lemonade and sunshine are awfully important around here.

More tongue hanging out than a bunch of blue-tick hounds at a meat market—When a man sees a beautiful woman, he looks like a dog that's drooling over a pork chop at Mr. Sammy's Butcher Shop!

Nailing jelly to a tree—Have you ever tried this? Impossible!

Panties in a bunch—Upset.

Smooth as butter—A person who is naturally good at charming people

Spit can—A used coffee cup, cola bottle, or an empty can that a Southern boy uses to spit the juice from the tobacco he is so elegantly (not!) chewing. It's not a pretty sight!

So dumb she needs instructions to climb a ladder—Um, who needs instructions to climb a ladder? See what I mean?

Squeal like a stuck pig—Yelling loudly. If you've ever stuck a pig, you know!

Sweet as a jug of iced tea—Um, did you read the recipe chapter?

That dog won't hunt—That just won't do!

There's always more silk blouses—There's always another of whatever it is you're looking for.

Thick as bricks—*See* Dumber than a bucket of rocks.

Tu-tu—Down "there."

Where in tarnation?—Where in the hell?

Whippersnapper—A "go get 'em" kind of person, usually young.

ACKNOWLEDGMENTS

Where do I start? Bear with me because there are a few people I couldn't have done this without.

To my wonderfully witty husband, Jim, who was always willing to sit with me, have a drink (or two), and give me great material for the book. You not only make me a happy girl, but boy, can you make me laugh!

To my dear friend, Mary Jane, who edited every single word for me as a favor. She never missed a chance to make my book better or to tell me my writing sucked at any particular juncture. Plus, if you ever get the opportunity to meet her, she is the most hysterical girl I know! She is a true friend, and I couldn't imagine not knowing her.

To my mother, whom we affectionately have nicknamed Diamond Lil, because she is known for her love of jewelry. She is the quintessential Southern belle. She is a great mother and a wonderful friend. She has blushed at many things in this book, and even asked if I shouldn't use a pseudonym! But she has always been supportive and a great fan.

To dozens of others, but I'll only name a few. To Anne, Michelle, Beth, Sarah, Brooke, and Mary Kay. Despite my having to ply you with liquor, your stories were hilarious, and some of my best stuff came from those cocktail hours. I'm about as lucky a girl I know to have such a great posse!

Last, but absolutely not least, to June, my agent, and Danielle, my editor at Citadel, for taking the risk with an inexperienced Southern belle and watching my back every step of the way!